A racy and rumbustious clerical autobiography ~~.... .. ....~~
reflective swansong of a distinguished religious broadcaster.

Harry Reid, former Editor, The Herald.

*Be warned! This book does not keep its distance. It will get under
your skin. It is passionately committed and achingly honest. That's
as personal as it gets.*

Revd Alan McDonald, Moderator designate of the General
Assembly of 2006

A Touch Personal

A Touch Personal
Life in the worlds
of faith and broadcasting

Johnston McKay

Shoving Leopard

Published by
Shoving Leopard
8 Edina Street (2f3)
Edinburgh,
EH2 5PN,
Scotland

http://www.shovingleopard.com

Cover design: Context Edinburgh T:07952 184 166
Cover photograph: Davide Metzger

ISBN 1-905565-06-2 Paperback

Dedication

For
John Fitzsimmons
who proves that integrity matters more than success

and for
the congregations of Barony St John's and Canonmills
who have proved that size doesn't matter

Foreword

The book in your hands is alive! Turn the pages and you will meet real people, dilemmas you'll probably recognise in your own life and ideas that are embodied in stories and passion.

The man and his story operate on a broad canvas. Starting in a manse in the chocolate-box surroundings of Perthshire, you travel widely. The High Kirk of St Giles in Edinburgh and Paisley Abbey provide distinguished settings for a few of the chapters but some of Johnston McKay's most fulfilling work was done for congregations in Glasgow and Ardrossan. Cambridge University sharpened his mind and the BBC fostered his instinctive skills of communication. Follow him to the Sea of Galilee, or the lair of an official of Hamas, to Ground Zero and to a poor AIDS clinic in a South African township.

Stories tumble over each other in the book as they do in his conversation. He approaches life alert to the pictures that words convey and the humorous potential of it all. Stories explain things you thought you understood. They take you behind the scenes of staid institutions. They lighten serious messages and point up the significance of everyday experiences. Parables have an honourable pedigree in this world.

And the people! Johnston has known many of Scotland's key churchmen of the last fifty years and there are anecdotes aplenty about them. But the ones that stay with you are the elder with the steely glare who complains about all that talk about Christianity when they really want to talk about the church, or the sad phone call from a gay man who was feeling the church's rejection painfully.

Carrying you through the book is the drive and the honesty of someone who has always had a passion about communicating the Christian message and has done so from the pulpit, with a microphone and in action. He will share with you his excitement about this message and the struggles he has gone through to understand it better. He makes a clear distinction between that message and the various vehicles for transmitting it – the church, the radio programme, the local congregation. These vehicles are analysed intensely, and you discover the roots of his frustration with the church, yet his love of it; the expansive vision of how radio can draw people into familiarity with faith; and his close engagement with the people, the pain and the little satisfactions of congregational life.

Getting to know Johnston McKay is a precious thing. He holds in tension various characteristics. He is instinctively generous, yet someone who has fierce loyalties; he is used to making his opinions public, yet prepared to change them; intellectually sharp, he spends time making his message simple and vivid. He lives a full life and, in this book, the reader can get a taste of it. I hope you enjoy it.

Alison Elliot
November, 2005

Introduction

The young woman in the mobile telephone shop was trying to tell me all the things my new, upgraded phone could do. One of the things was that I could load photographs of everyone in my contact list into the phone so that when I spoke to them the photograph would appear. "But I know what people in my list look like" I said. My wife, Evelyn, smiled mischievously, and after a slight pause said, lovingly, "But for how long Johnston?"

I don't know for how long some of the memories in this book will stay clear and vivid, but over the years, as I've shared them with people, some of them have said "You should write them down". So I have: not just because they are stories from my time in the church and the BBC, but because I realise now that what we believe is best communicated through story.

I want to thank those who have most intimately shared my story: Evelyn and Cally, Kevin and Robert who have indulged the religious convictions I have but made sure that they were kept in their place; and my sister Thea and brother Ralston with whom I have come through a lot. They matter much more than you would know from what follows.

I owe the title of this book to Douglas Alexander, who suggested it after we had a very pleasant lunch together. He and his wife Joyce, along with Tom and Pat McWilliam, Andrew and Irene McLellan and Martin and Irene Doole made sure I survived intact. There are those who may not thank them for ensuring my survival, but I am not one of them!

Alison Elliot not only contributed the very generous foreword but when she saw the first draft of this book, suggested ways in which she, very wisely, thought it could be improved. She was right. That is just one of the debts I owe to her. The others can't be easily acknowledged because they are inextricably tied up in the way I now think about faith, God, society and the church's place in it. I am very glad that a proposal I made in the General Assembly in the 1970s that the Church and Nation committee should be thanked and discharged was unsuccessful: not the first or last time that I was wrong at the wrong time!

When I first showed the manuscript to Janet de Vigne I did not know how she would react. Her enthusiasm for the book has been very important, and encouraged me to work far harder at getting it ready for publication than I otherwise would have done.

Johnston McKay
Advent 2005

1

It was the summer of 1961.

I was spending the university holiday with my uncle and aunt in the parish of Kenmore, where my uncle Kenneth was the minister. I had just finished my first year, and had passed only in History. I had failed English and Latin. I was not surprised I had failed the Latin because I had not turned up to sit it!

So in the manse of Kenmore, with its many rooms and its large garden, overlooking Loch Tay with Ben Lawers in the distance, still flecked with snow even though this was the height of summer, I spent the months from June until September, visiting some of my uncle's scattered flock. On Sundays I took services in neighbouring churches. The rest of the time I was studying English.

Earlier in the year my uncle Kenneth and aunt Isabel had welcomed a fourth child into their family: my little cousin Jean. Her christening was celebrated with a huge party and much champagne. In my case, too much champagne. The story goes that I was last seen draped over the style which led to the hen house, on my way to shut in the manse hens for the night. I have no memory of that, or of anything else that evening. I do remember, however, waking up the following morning with an extremely sore head. Through the opened window of the attic where I slept, I could hear my uncle clipping the garden hedge. Suddenly he let out a scream, followed by some choice expletives, a few of which owed their origin to early Anglo-Saxon. Even as I opened the skylight window to ask him why he was cutting the hedge at what seemed an unearthly hour in the morning, I realised what he had done: he had confirmed me in my decision to become a minister. If my uncle Kenneth, a respected parish minister, could curse like that when he cut his finger, there was no reason why I should continue to harbour the fear that I was not good enough to be a Church of Scotland minister!

One of the reasons I had gone to Kenmore was to study for the examinations I had to re-sit, having failed two out of three in May. Unlike today's students who have to find the money themselves to pay fees and live, I had what was called a university grant, which paid for my tuition and also the cost of upkeep. Not unnaturally the grant authority expected students to pass, and unless two out of three subjects in the first year were passed, the grant would be withheld. Unless I was able, in the quaint phrase used at the time "to satisfy the examiners", I would have to leave. I scraped a pass in English, and so began my second year.

My distinct lack of academic success was due to spending almost all my time in the debating chamber of the university union. I thoroughly enjoyed both the company and the debating jousts of those days with students who were far better debaters that I would ever be: people like John Smith and Donald Dewar, Menzies Campbell and John MacKay, Neil McCormick and David Miller. I enjoyed their company. I basked in their reflections. And I was beginning to pass examinations. Things were looking up. I had worked out how to spend time debating and in academic study.

One Sunday afternoon, towards the end of the debating season in March, I was in the Students' Union with two much older students and much more experienced debaters, John Smith, who went on to lead the Labour Party, and Malcolm Mackenzie, a Tory who became a very important figure in the world of Scottish education. I can't remember how the conversation got round to the future, but both of them told me, quietly but firmly, that I wasn't clever enough to combine debating with academic work and succeed at both, and they thought I didn't have enough common sense to realise that getting a degree was more important than succeeding in debates.

The next day I decided to abandon the university's student life, to give up the debating at which I was never as good as I thought, and concentrate on getting a degree. Two years later I graduated with a second class honours degree in Politics and Modern History.

So, now married to Heather, whom I had met in the world of university debating, and fallen in love with very quickly, I began a course in theology at St John's College in Cambridge.

The idea was not at first mine. My father was a very well-known minister, not only in Glasgow, but in the Church of Scotland. I knew that wherever in Scotland I prepared for the ministry, I would always be my father's son, unable to escape from his shadow. When I talked to the late Professor William Barclay about this, he asked why I did not think about going to Cambridge. His great friend, Charlie Moule, was a teacher there, and a Fellow of Clare College, and he would see what Professor Moule could do. So I prepared an application to study at the University of Cambridge, which is structured as a number of colleges. When asked for my first choice of college, I naturally chose Professor Moule's Clare College. I knew nothing about any of the other colleges, which I had to list in order of preference, but I noticed that the Master of St John's College was a clergyman called Boys Smith and that seemed a good enough reason for making St John's my second choice of college.

What I did not know was that Professor Moule had very little influence on which applicants his college chose, and that it seldom chose very many to study theology. But, shortly after a letter of rejection from Clare College came a letter from St John's, offering me a place and asking me to present myself at the college at the beginning of October 1965. This time, I was determined that there would be no repeat of academic failure.

The great Scottish reformer John Knox had sent his two sons to St John's College in Cambridge, and they lie buried today just outside the south wall of the college chapel. But the Church of Scotland in the 1960s was a lot more suspicious of Cambridge than Knox was in the fifteen sixties. I was told that in order to keep me in touch with "the Presbyterian tradition", I should enrol as an attached student at Westminster College, the seminary for training ministers of the Presbyterian Church of England.

Friday evenings were special in Westminster College. Each of the second and third year students was expected to conduct worship and preach in the college chapel, to a congregation of all the students and staff. Then dinner was served, and afterwards the entire gathering made its way to the college common room where the four professors sat in a row facing the students, sitting round the walls of the common room with the preacher on a chair on his own in the middle of the room. One by one the professors delivered a critique of the service. I can think of no experience in my life which was more frightening, or more valuable. If, as a parish minister, I made rigorous and thorough sermon preparation an absolute priority, I owe it to those Friday evening sermon criticisms, one of which was "led" by the Professor of New Testament then at Westminster, John O'Neill, who later moved to the chair of New Testament in the University of Edinburgh, and to whose teaching and friendship I owe an un-repayable debt. His death in 2003 was a dreadful blow, and taking part in his funeral service was an enormous privilege.

My principal academic home, however, was St John's College, where I had the huge good fortune to have, as a director of studies, a young theologian, not much older than myself, but who by then had collected first class honours degrees from Cambridge, Oxford and Harvard. Stephen Sykes was later to become Professor of Theology at Durham, Oxford and Cambridge and then Bishop of Ely. Not even Stephen's kindly direction was able to prepare me for the culture shock of moving from a university like Glasgow, where the basic method of teaching was the lectures – which I eventually accepted I had to attend and learn from – to a place like Cambridge, where what mattered was a student's weekly essay, written for and read to a supervisor. I still recall being told on my very first day that I was to start working on the Old Testament, and that I would be taught by a Franciscan called Barnabas Lindars. So, as instructed, I called to see him and he handed me a piece of paper on which he had written the question "Who wrote the Psalms?" and then a few books which I should start reading. "Come back at the same time next week and read me a 2000 word essay on the subject". In a daze I made my way back to our flat. I knew absolutely nothing about who might or might not have written the Psalms, when or where they might have been written, and why it mattered. But within a week I had started to learn, and to learn in the way that gave me a real 'buzz' on my own with books.

There were lectures "offered" by the university and some I made a point of always attending. Professor Dennis Nineham's lectures on the Gospels were brilliantly captivating. Many years later he agreed to take part in a series of radio programmes I produced about the bible called "It ain't necessarily so". By then he had retired to Oxford, and I arrived at his house to record his contribution. As we drank coffee before the recording, I reminded him that at the end of his last lecture to us he said something like this: "Four times a week for two terms you have listened to me talking about the Gospels. You have heard me say, time and again, that they are not biographies of Jesus. You will shortly write examination answers explaining that the Gospels cannot provide us with biographical information about Jesus. And in a few years' time, if I visit the parishes of those of you who are going to be ordained, I will doubtless hear you preaching sermons on the life of Jesus according to the Gospels". I silently vowed that in the unlikely event of the professor turning up at a church where I was preaching, he would be proved wrong!

As in most university courses there were optional modules. At Cambridge one of these was Hebrew, whereas, had I studied at a Scottish university Hebrew would have been compulsory. Before moving south, I wrote to the Education for the Ministry committee of the Church of Scotland, saying that I intended to study at Cambridge and enclosing a copy of the two year course of study with all the options listed. Was there anything which the Church required me to study which might not be compulsory within the degree course? The reply came back from the Secretary of the committee saying that there was no particular part of the course which the committee stipulated must be undertaken: just complete a degree.

However, a few months before I was due to sit my final examinations, I received a letter from the committee expressing some concern that there was no Hebrew component in my course and that in the light of this the committee was not sure my Cambridge degree was acceptable as the equivalent of two of the three years required in academic training for the ministry. There followed a long exchange of letters, in the course of which I was told that the Secretary should not have told me what I should do, but eventually I was advised that if I applied under some section or other of the regulations I would be excused Hebrew. I wrote off the letter and then looked up the passage in the regulations to which I had been directed to refer in my letter. I discovered that I was to be excused Hebrew "on the grounds of failing eyesight"!

I worked very, very hard at Cambridge, but as May 1967 and the seven finals papers got closer, I became very anxious. There was so much I had not covered properly. The final examinations were spread over three and a half days, two three hour papers each day until the final morning when there was what was called "the essay": a choice of, I think eight topics, and for three hours an essay on one of them had to be written.

With each exam paper that I sat I became more depressed. On the night before the essay I phoned home and told my father not to make any arrangements to come to Cambridge for the graduation. I had done so badly that I expected only to scrape the poorest degree, and that would be nothing to celebrate.

When I looked at the topics for the final general essay, I couldn't believe my luck: one of the essays was to be a discussion of whether the religion of protestants is solely based on the bible. I had prepared a talk for the college theological society on a very similar subject just a few months earlier, and I could still remember off by heart a lot of the quotations used on both sides of the argument. I started writing and virtually reproduced the talk I had prepared. I knew the essay was excellent. Maybe it might just push me off the bottom grade of degree.

Three weeks later, at ten o'clock in the morning, the examination results were posted on the notice board on the wall of the university Senate House. After frantically searching for my name in all the categories I thought it most likely to be, and failing to find it, I turned to a Kevin Lewis, an American with whom I had become very friendly. "My name's not there" I said. "Yes it is. You've got a bloody first!"

The next day I went to see Stephen Sykes in his rooms in College. As a young university teacher then, I was the first "first" he had pass through his hands. He said to me that he was sure that if I wanted, the college would make it possible for me to stay on and do research in preparation for what he now assumed would be an academic career. But I was determined to return to Scotland, and take up a post I had been offered as assistant minister at St Giles' Cathedral in Edinburgh.

The preparation which the Church of Scotland had expected me to go through, and at the time expected all divinity students to go through, and the ministry we entered, seems light years away from today.

First of all there has been a huge change in the academic standard expected of those entering the ministry. Gone is the necessity to study the bible in the original languages. The knowledge of church history expected is sketchy, unless it is being taken as an honours subject. The attention paid to the early period of theology, say until the middle of the fifth century − which was so determinative of all that was later to be said and taught − is very limited. The result of this is clear; it was predicted by some of us, as soon as we began to see the church choosing the attractive but slippery course of lowering academic standards in order to maintain the number of candidates for the ministry: something it has signally failed to do. With some notable exceptions, the Church of Scotland is unable to provide from its own ranks scholars of ability who could, in time, become the teachers of the next generation.

People of real ability will not become ministers if the training they receive is not challenging, and what is expected of today's ministers in training, academically, is poor. There has been considerable attention paid to improving the practical training students receive, and far more supervision of the places where they gain practical expertise. And there has been a radical improvement in the training of those parish ministers who can expect to have students working with them, or graduates sent to them for their final eighteen month placement, and all of that is laudable. But as the church has dictated to the universities what it wants divinity students to learn, the universities have responded by delivering what is expected.

When Colin MacIntosh, now the minister of Dunblane Cathedral, was inducted to his first parish in Glasgow, the minister preaching at the presbytery service, not a graduate himself, told Colin − who had a first class honours degree from Glasgow − that the Church was "dying by degrees". Many years later, by then in the BBC, I had the opportunity to see at first hand Colin's dealing with the awful consequences of Thomas Hamilton's massacre in Dunblane's primary school. I will take a lot of convincing that the way he dealt both with the bereaved and with the effect of his own involvement did not owe a great deal to the academic training which taught him to reflect deeply, rigorously and theologically about the events he was caught up in. The sermon he preached on the Sunday after the massacre was a model both of pastoral sensitivity and theological depth. If, today, not much is demanded of divinity students, not very much will be learned.

The year I returned to after my two years in Cambridge contained people of the calibre of Andrew McLellan and Sandy Macdonald, both of them moderators of the General Assembly, James Miller, who had distinguished ministries in Peterhead, Dumbarton and Dunblane Cathedral before leaving Scotland for the United States, Bob Brown, who served the church outstandingly both in pastoral ministries and important committees, David Graham, whose flair and ability was such that he was able to capture the imagination of Glasgow presbytery, David Lunan, now the clerk of Glasgow presbytery. Now? Hardly any in each year.

However, unlike the situation facing today's divinity students, the ministry I entered was one whose future seemed assured. There was a pattern of ministry which was accepted almost without question. A minister would be expected to preach, normally twice a Sunday, and visit the congregation in their homes at least once after arriving in the parish. Some might visit the whole congregation regularly; others would see their priority as visiting the old and the housebound. If faithfully followed, that pattern of ministry would ensure that the congregation survived and the Church of Scotland's role as the national church continued.

There were very few who noticed that the membership of

the Church had begun slowly to decline from its peak. The haemorrhaging of the membership was then a cloud no bigger than a man's hand. We now know that the time when the kirk's membership reached its peak, in the 1950s, was a remarkable time politically in Scotland. The 1955 General Election was the last occasion when any party won more than 50% of the vote, and it was the Tory Party. The Scotland which gave the Church of Scotland its highest membership was a very conservative Scotland. Since that peak year, the Church of Scotland's political stance has become increasingly left-wing, and it has lost support. I suspect the reason is that the part of Scotland whose political conservatism was reflected in a comfortable, conservative church has dramatically declined, as that Scotland now has only one Conservative member of the Westminster parliament, and left wing Scotland has been reflected in a more left wing church. But a left wing Scotland was a lot less interested in the Church.

Nor were there very many recognising what Callum Brown has drawn attention to in his study of *The Death of Christian Britain*, that the Church of Scotland of the mid-1950s had been unquestioningly male dominated, and the gradual liberation of women from the subservient role, to which both society and church condemned them, was inevitably going to decrease the influence of the Church, so reflective as it was of a male dominated society. When she was moderator of the General Assembly, Alison Elliot said that Callum Brown's book was one which had a tremendously powerful effect on her precisely because it showed her that the much lauded good old days, of the Church of Scotland's so-called finest hour, were ones to which she would not wish to return.

Nor were there very many in those days, when I was preparing to enter the ministry, questioning whether the church had depended for its continued impact on a population which was relatively static. Increased mobility, the renewal of the urban environment, the creation of sprawling housing schemes and new towns posed challenges which the church thought it could meet by replicating the pattern of church life and work which had existed for almost a century.

Forty years earlier, the visionary George MacLeod had sensed that a change was overtaking Scotland and had founded his Iona Community, to encourage a different form and style of ministry which he knew was necessary, even if he himself was not temperamentally suited to undertake it. More recently, the equally visionary Geoff Shaw had inspired the Gorbals Group, which had also struggled to find a way of being a church which suited changing times. But just as George MacLeod's community had met with at best suspicion and at worst contempt, so the suggestion from the Gorbals Group that traditional patterns of church life were becoming increasingly irrelevant was at best patronised and at worst dismissed out of hand. I remember vividly a television programme, in which the minister of a very comfortable suburban church talked about the future with John Harvey, then a young minister involved with the Gorbals Group. The effortless condescension of the experienced minister is something which has stayed with me ever since.

I have often reflected on why it is that the Church of Scotland, which takes pride in the claim that it is "reformed but always in need of reformation" is so slow to recognise when change is necessary and so resistant to adopting anything which breaks traditional moulds.

There may be many reasons, but two lie at the root of the kirk's conservatism.

Suspicion of change is built into the structure and ethos of the Church of Scotland. All of those who operate at its centre accept the premise that the Church is basically a legal entity, which must operate in a way consistent with its legal framework. The only way to change the church, therefore, is to change the legal framework. But the legal framework can only be changed by the General Assembly, which is representative of those who are least likely to embrace radical change. And those who operate the Church's legal structures are willing only to promote or accept changes which can be accommodated within the legal structure. However, there may be other ways of being a church which do not assume that going by some rule book is inherently the only way to proceed.

The second reason for the kirk's conservatism is doubtless shared by other institutions, the tendency for permanent officials to absorb the protests of transient radicals, or else the tendency of the transient radicals to become part of the system. All of us who have thought we had a radical vision for the church, or reforms which we believe are necessary, have convinced ourselves that the way to make the vision a reality, or to bring about the reforms, is to work within the existing structures. However the existing structures are temptingly alluring, and the radical visionary or the institutional reformer soon recognises the difficulties and problems which lie between him or her and the impossible dream, and so begins to settle for the achievable targets rather than the ever moving horizon. If you stay outside the system in order to preserve the clarity of your critique you will be accused of irresponsibly denying to the church your insights, but the moment you succumb to that flattering judgment, you will find your insights being compromised.

There is one other great difference between the ministry today and the ministry of forty years ago. Then it was assumed that the ministry of word and sacrament was the form of ministry which mattered more than any other. And I have to confess that I bought into that view, and not always for the best of motives. I won't have been the only person who found that view of the ministry attractive, because it provided a sense not just of importance but of indispensability which was psychologically necessary. Over the years I have come to realise that it was theological nonsense. I wish, however, that some other word than "ministry" could be used to describe the shared responsibility all of us have for being the church. I suspect that as the "ministry" in which everyone is involved, or of different roles within the paid service of the church, which has recently been acknowledged in the creation of a "Ministries Council", recognising that the diaconate, parish assistants, youth workers, bereavement counsellors and a host of other professionals are as much ministries as that of those who wear dog collars, has been, rightly, stressed, so the ordained ministry of word and sacrament has become increasingly unsure of why it exists.

2

In the 1960s, the ministers of the kirk's prestigious charges cherry-picked assistants from the supply of final year divinity students, sometimes on the basis of academic record, sometimes on the old boy network. So, after a year of study in the United States, Andrew McLellan went as assistant minister to St George's West in Edinburgh, and Bob Brown became assistant in the capital's suburban Greenbank. Jim Miller became assistant in St John's Kirk of Perth. So there was nothing out of the ordinary in Harry Whitley, the minister of St Giles' Cathedral, suggesting to my father that I would be the ideal young minister to be his assistant.

Harry had a maverick track record in his recent appointments of assistants. He had appointed the Anglican John Tirrell, who was a postgraduate student at Edinburgh University. When the Anglicans declined to support Tirrell exercising a full ministry at St Giles (i.e. a ministry which celebrated the Sacrament of the Lord's Supper) first the presbytery of Edinburgh and then the General Assembly refused to support Harry Whitley. John Tirrell had decided to leave Edinburgh and vacate the flat he had enjoyed to his successor, Johnston McKay.

I joined the staff of St Giles in October 1967. The other two assistants were a German Lutheran called Dieter de Lazzer, and an American Presbyterian from Baltimore, Bill Hill. Both of them, I recall, had turned up to worship in St Giles, been spotted as strangers and invited to lunch at the manse. Harry's wife Betty had the impossible task, each week, of preparing Sunday lunch, without having a clue how many people Harry would speak to at church and then ask them to the manse.

For nearly three years David Ogston and I were Harry Whitley's assistants: but more than that, together we ran the public side of the cathedral while Harry increasingly spent time in his country retreat in Galloway. He was tired, exhausted by the battles he had to fight in St Giles, and reluctant, now that these battles had all been won, to abandon either the pulpit of St Giles, or the role of Dean of the Order of the Thistle, to which he had been appointed following the death of his predecessor at St Giles in 1969.

So David and I learned our trade "on the hoof". I recall one Sunday morning in the vestry of St Giles'. As usual the suave organist Herrick Bunney came in about 10.30 a m to check the hymns he and Harry had discussed the night before. "We've got the Twenty Third Psalm this morning" said Herrick. "Yes, yes, yes" said Harry "and I think we should sing it to the tune Crimond. I haven't sung 'The Lord's my Shepherd' to Crimond for ages". There was a brief pause, and from the corner of the vestry David Ogston muttered "If the old man ever went to a crematorium he'd sing the Twenty-Third Psalm to Crimond"!

Because Harry Whitley relied heavily on his assistants, St Giles' introduced me to church politics and ecclesiastical politics at a level which a young assistant could not have imagined being involved in; and, if truth be told, at a level at which a young assistant minister should not have been involved in.

But I was, and it was all grist to the mill of a young minister who had the washing-powdered gleam of the moderatorial lace in his distant sights!

Harry Whitley's ministry in St Giles' had been a difficult one. Called to be colleague and successor to the courtly Charles Warr, whom King George V had described as his "boy dean" when he appointed him to be Dean of the Thistle and the Chapel Royal, he found Dr Warr unwilling to take the back seat that he had promised to take, when he wrote in the St Giles' parish magazine following Harry's induction, that Dr Whitley "as moderator of the kirk session is henceforth in charge of the parish and congregation. In future, therefore, all requests regarding baptism, marriages, sick visits, and all matters connected with the organisation and activities of the congregation must be addressed to Dr Whitley at the Manse in the first instance."

For more than ten years Dr Warr and his friends within the congregation, and in the many Edinburgh societies and organisations with which he had connections, made the life of the minister of St Giles' very difficult. Of that there is no doubt. There is equally no doubt in my mind – much as I loved him and owe him an enormous amount – that Harry's tendency to view life as a series of conspiracies did not help the situation, and his habit of impetuously regarding every issue in which he felt slighted as of equal importance and a challenge, not just to his own ministry but to the church's fundamental understanding of the role of a parish minister often exacerbated disagreements and allowed them to expand out of all proportion. However, having expressed that judgment I have to acknowledge that I have not experienced the slights, hurts, insults and criticism which he did, but I have enjoyed the warmth, extreme generosity, wonderful company and affirming confidence which he gave to his assistants.

I came to St Giles' as a replacement for the American Anglican John Tirrell whom Harry had asked to be his assistant. Tirrell's bishop agreed and the young persuasive American started work. The trouble arose when Harry wanted his young assistant to celebrate the Lord's Supper. That required the permission of the presbytery of Edinburgh about which Harry had not always been polite. Its members included some staunch supporters of the movement for church unity, who felt that Harry Whitley, no supporter of institutional ecumenical moves, was at best endangering the gradual process towards unity and at worst deliberately scuppering it. The presbytery of Edinburgh, on a recount after a vote of 106 in favour of the young assistant to 105 against , voted 106 against and 105 for. Another recount produced a vote of 106 each way. The moderator of presbytery asked if the matter could be referred to the General Assembly rather than resolved by his casting vote. The General Assembly, disliking bucks being passed to it, sent the matter back to the presbytery of Edinburgh which agreed that Tirrell could celebrate the sacraments so long as his bishop in America and the Bishop of Edinburgh agreed. However the presbytery knew very well that Kenneth Carey, the Bishop of Edinburgh, was not going to agree. The plan was dropped and shortly afterwards a disillusioned John Tirrell left St Giles'.

The story of what became well known as "the Tirrell Affair" received a huge amount of publicity, particular in the Scottish Daily Express which revelled in what it could portray as a struggle between the minister of St Giles' and bishops. Earlier that year, it had carried a series of articles alleging that enthusiastic ecumenicals in the Church of Scotland had gone far beyond the remit given to them in Anglican-Presbyterian conversations, and were proposing a union of churches which would involve a mutual recognition of ministries, but all future ordinations would have involved an Episcopal element. It quoted leaked documents which supported the allegations.

The articles had been written by Professor Ian Henderson, who subsequently described both the conversations and the Tirrell affair in his very controversial book *Power without Glory*. The themes, of relationships with the Church of England, and of church committees exceeding their remits and powers, were ones which I turned to when a completely unexpected invitation arrived from the Editor of *The Glasgow Herald*, inviting me to become the Herald's Church Correspondent. The editor, Alastair Warren, wrote "I do feel that we need to have someone of about your age who will not allow the congregation to fall asleep. The duties are not onerous, involving two articles a month and additional pieces occasionally."

Some of the articles I had written in the St Giles parish

magazine, the *St Giles' News*, had attracted some attention in the secular press. One had poked some fun at the moderator's gaiters, his requiring two chaplains and his title as a "right reverend". Another summed up a meeting of the General Assembly as "tired and dull".

In October 1968 I had written an article for *The Glasgow Herald* headlined "How they choose a moderator" which caused an amount of controversy when it was published, five days before the meeting of the committee, which that year nominated the Glasgow minister Dr Tom Murchison. At the meeting, the chairman, Dr Archie Watt criticised the article, and the former moderator, Dr John Fraser, expressed his regret that there seemed to be no way the Church could discipline the article's author. The editor of the Herald wrote to me that he thought it "a first class piece and it caused quite a stir in one or two quarters".

I was encouraged by the editor's letter to think that I might be able to write from time to time. I had been interested in journalism ever since, along with two other sons of the manse, Michael Mair, now a minister in Dundee, and John MacBeath, now a professor in Cambridge, I had edited in my sixth year at the High School of Glasgow, a school newspaper which was sufficiently interesting to be banned by the Head Teacher. However it had never crossed my mind that I might be invited to become a correspondent for *The Glasgow Herald*. I realised from the editor's response to what I had previously written for the Herald that what prompted the invitation to me was not any brilliance in my literary style, nor the power of my investigative journalism, but an ability to provoke reaction which either sustained a story or invited contributions to the letters column. So the first article I wrote was deliberately provocative. Drawing on the recent news that the Queen, the following year, was to attend the General Assembly herself rather than appoint a Lord High Commissioner, it reflected on the implication if the head of the Church of England attended, as her Lord High Commissioner always did, the Assembly's Communion Service in St Giles' Cathedral at a time when the Church of England's official position could be construed as questioning the validity of that communion service.

The article was taken up not just by letter writers to *The Herald* but by other Scottish newspapers, such as *The Daily Express* ("The Kirk and the Queen's Communion") and *The Daily Record* ("Hark the Herald [and Express] Angels Sing") and by religious journals such as the now defunct *British Weekly* and *New Christian*.

The second article I wrote, headed "Rights of presbytery taken over by Church" described the unease felt by congregations at financial targets for contributions to the church's work set by the kirk's bureaucrats and the increasing role of the central administration in the approval of candidates for the ministry. I have to say that I could not have dreamed of how far in the direction of centralisation the church of the twenty first century would have gone! Two weeks later I revealed that a proposal that representatives of the Church of Scotland and the Episcopal Church in Scotland should sit on each other's committees, which was to be submitted to the General Assembly a few years later, had already been discussed and approved by the Church and Nation committee. I reported that a number of members of the Church and Nation committee had complained that the proposal had not been fully discussed, and that it had not been approved in the form it appeared in the committee's minute, which I quoted.

Again the issues were taken up by other newspapers, and in the letters column. Less publicly the acting Principal Clerk of the General Assembly wrote a personal letter to the editor of *The Herald*, expressing fears about "a serious breach of good relations between *The Glasgow Herald* and the Church of Scotland", and Andrew Herron, as Clerk to Glasgow presbytery wrote to the editor complaining that as a journalist I was entitled to use whatever information came my way but as a minister (he clearly by then knew who "our churches correspondent" was) I was bound to honour any seal of confidentiality imposed on a document by a committee of the church. This was not a view to which he had subscribed, however, when he enthusiastically supported Professor Ian Henderson's leaking of documents in connection with the Anglican-Presbyterian conversations. Andrew Herron continued "Had I reason to believe your correspondent was under the care of this presbytery I assure you this fact would have been very vividly brought to his notice long ere this." Ironically, several years later, when I was a minister in Glasgow presbytery, Andrew Herron was to invite me to become the editor of the presbytery's newspaper, *The Bush*.

For the next two years I continued to write a fortnightly column for the Herald, not very many of which produced the storm of protest aroused by these early articles but which continued to be provocative and were intended, often, as good "knockabout stuff". They took a very simplistic view of the Church and frequently exaggerated a case. Of course I outgrew some of the prejudices they reflected (and doubtless gathered some others!) and began to reflect more critically on the church for myself rather than be convinced by strong influences on me like my father, Harry Whitley and Professor Ian Henderson. However although I recognise now the immaturity of many of the views expressed in these articles I am not prepared totally to dissociate myself from them. The philosopher Alasdair MacIntyre once commented, sharply but very perceptively, that "power compromises and absolute power compromises absolutely". At the time I wrote regularly for *The Glasgow Herald*, I was young, inexperienced and had no experience of the power structures of the Church. So my views had not yet succumbed to the inevitable compromises that involvement in decision-making always brings. But I was young, and the young don't know that yet. The first speech I ever made at a presbytery meeting was an instinctive protest against something which I thought was wrong, and began "moderator, I am young, so I am still young enough to be shocked ...!" I grew up and learned by experience the truth of the maxim that there are only two types of people: the pure and the responsible. But as I look back on the controversies I contributed to in those days just after I was ordained, and from whence I acquired the reputation for being an angry young man, I reflect on two things.

It is, I think, extremely sad, and not to the benefit of the church, that there seem to be no angry young ministers today, with sufficient passion to speak out, or enough love for the church to owe it their outspokenness. There are probably a number of reasons for this. An apparently rigorous selection process, which was once rather wickedly described as being designed "to separate the chaff from the chaff" may possibly eradicate people who demonstrate a combative personality or who are not afraid to express strong views. The sort of signals which young ministers are given by the church about what sort of leaders it expects its ministers to grow into may have changed. When I was a young minister, men like John R Gray of Dunblane, Bill Johnston of Colinton and the scholar Robin Barbour were preparing to take over the leadership of the church from powerful, charismatic figures like Hugh Douglas, Leonard Small, and still there, brooding over them all, the ageing but ever magnetic personality of George MacLeod; all of them in very different but powerful ways conveying the impression that they had a vision for the church, and to be the church meant having a vision that was inspiring. You might not agree with the vision, but you were in no doubt the "vision thing" was an important aspect of their leadership qualities.

Today's church leaders, with some notable exceptions seem replicas of business middle managers, concerned with administrative detail, pragmatic policies, efficient bureaucracy.

On the first occasion when I preached at a presbytery service, as the most recently inducted minister whose turn it was, I said on that occasion that the great danger for the church was that in seeking to organise itself efficiently it was in danger of substituting targets for horizons. Afterwards I heard Andrew Herron, just returned to his duties as presbytery Clerk from his year as moderator, sigh wearily and say to someone that when he became presbytery Clerk he thought he would get lots of ideas for sermons from the ones he had to hear at presbytery services, but he was always disappointed! I sense today even more than I did thirty years ago that those in positions of responsibility and influence in the church are more concerned with achieving targets within the church than with reaching out towards horizons for God's people. Pragmatism is more important than passion, and pragmatism as a model doesn't inspire young ministers to be rebellious.

And, of course, fewer and fewer of the new entrants to the ministry are as young as I and my contemporaries were: just through school and universities. Today's entrants come in much later, after other careers, perhaps where the lessons of compromise have already been learned or where idealism and passion have been found not to pay the mortgage.

Meanwhile, in St Giles', I was undertaking the normal duties of a probationary assistant minister, visiting members of the congregation, taking weddings, conducting funerals, and Sunday by Sunday taking part in worship.

My first, and mind-blowing, impression of worship in St Giles' Cathedral was of the music. The sheer power of the organ took my breath away. The stunning range of the choir's repertoire was so exciting. I had never experienced the power of music in worship before, and its effect was exhilarating. Most Sundays, Harry Whitley preached and one of the assistants conducted the service and led the congregation in prayer.

Harry Whitley was a compelling preacher, gripping and

entertaining when he was riding one of his many hobby-horses: concern for the environment (long before ecology was fashionable), self-government for Scotland (while I was an assistant, his wife Betty was an SNP candidate), protection of Scotland's rural communities (especially after he and his wife purchased a smallholding in rural Galloway) and the erosion of the powers of Scotland's local authorities (especially galling to him was the absorption of the burgh of Leith into the city of Edinburgh).

One Sunday morning I was with him as we made our way up the steps of the Cathedral, to be greeted by the most loyal of Harry's elders, an Edinburgh lawyer called Bertie Borland. He sighed as Bertie greeted him at the door, with "In good form this morning, Harry?" "No, no, no" muttered the minister of St Giles'. "I've only got half a sermon prepared". With a wide, mischievous smile, Bertie Borland retorted "Then preach the half you haven't prepared. They're always better".

After we had greeted the congregation at the door at the end of the service, and retired to the vestry to take off our ministerial robes, Harry used to listen for some word of encouraging comment from his assistants. If none was forthcoming he would always ask gently what had been wrong! One Sunday morning we all returned to the vestry; David Ogston and I busied ourselves, taking off our robes, hanging them up in the wardrobe, sorting our notes from the service and quite obviously making no comment on the sermon at all. After a little while Harry could stand it no longer. "Well, what did you think?" he asked almost pleadingly. We muttered something about it being quite a nice day outside. Harry turned to me. "Well what did you disagree with, Johnston?" I said, hesitantly, that I wasn't sure he should have made such an issue about 'thinking'. "What did I say about 'thinking'?" Harry asked. "Well", I answered, "you said that the trouble with the church today was there was far too much thinking for thinking's sake"! "Oh" grunted the minister of St Giles', making his way to his car.

Riding any of his hobby horses, Harry Whitley captured the attention of a congregation and always left people with something to think about. But his preaching was at its best, and at its best it had no equal, when he drew deeply on his well of suffering, pain and tortured hope. It was then that he built a bridge of shared experience between himself and his congregation on which faith could sometimes tiptoe and occasionally dance. Those sermons were dramatic encounters, when Harry virtually demanded that we come with him to the edge of despair, because he had been there and a thread of faith had held him from tumbling over, and he asked us to clutch with him that thread of faith.

I knew, then, as I listened, that this was authentic preaching as I had never heard it before. What I did not know then was that for the preaching to be authentic, you had to have been at the edge of despair, not just able to describe it.

When I started at St Giles, I assumed that prayers for Sunday services were read from a book. I had been introduced to various classic books of prayers in my training and I expected to make good use of them. Before the first service in which I took part Harry said that he expected his assistants to write their own prayers, and he expected them to spend as much time writing the prayers as he spent on a sermon. As far as I was concerned, his expectations were more than fulfilled! I would rather have written a dozen sermons than compose two prayers for a Sunday morning service. The struggle to find words that were both precise and ambiguous (because prayer is both specific and evocative) was something I will always be grateful that Harry demanded, for I had always assumed as a worshipper until then that I could switch off during prayers. The language was formal and involved me very little, whereas Harry kept insisting that the language had to be real: if it didn't embrace the congregation's own experience of living it would not involve them at all.

The first wedding I took in St Giles' is still vividly real. It was held in a side chapel, and I was concentrating carefully on every word I had to say, so carefully that for some time I did not realise that the bridegroom was swaying alarmingly from side to side. As I continued through the service the St Giles' beadle, a very large man called Jim McLaren, who in his days had been a Regimental Sergeant Major, indicated to the bride and the best man that they should move much closer to the 'groom to restrict his sidewards movement. However when they did this, the 'groom simply started swaying alarmingly backwards and forwards. At this point I began to be aware that something out of the ordinary was happening. From his position at the side of proceedings Jim McLaren muttered to me "Announce a hymn!" So I announced a hymn. "Get them to follow you into the vestry" he said, as the organist played over the opening lines of the hymn. So I motioned to the bridal party to follow me and we went into the vestry, where the ex RSM took over. "Off with your shoes!" he barked to the bridegroom, and as the white-faced groom started to remove his shoes and then his socks, and the hymn continued to be sung outside, Jim McLaren said to me "Old trick I learned in the army. If they're going to faint, get them to stand on a cold floor. All the blood will go to their feet and they'll stop feeling faint", and with that he formed the bridal party up and led them into the church, with its cold grey flagstones, where the bridegroom showed no further signs of either nervousness or light-headedness. When it was all over, however, it was the assistant minister who was in need of resuscitation!

Most of the weekly work provided the sort of experience an assistant would have gained whichever church or parish he had been assigned to. But because Harry increasingly came to rely on his assistants in situations which were unique to St Giles', the experience there was very different from the sort of issues with which assistants elsewhere had to deal.

There were special services regularly held in St Giles'. One of those was held each year on Battle of Britain Sunday in September. September was the month Harry Whitley always went on holiday, and so it was left to the assistants to arrange the service, rehearse those taking part, explain every year to the RAF colour party that it may well be the practice in the RAF church of St Clement Danes in London for the colour party to carry fixed bayonets, but they would not be doing that in St Giles'. For four years I conducted the Battle of Britain service, welcomed the congregation, announced the hymns, and said the prayers. But we always invited a veteran of the Battle of Britain or an RAF chaplain to preach the sermon. And after the service I was always invited to a splendid buffet lunch at RAF Pitreavie across the Forth Bridge. After the fourth of these services, and at the fourth lunch I attended, an RAF big-wig bearing more gold braid on his hat and shoulders than I had ever seen bore down on me.

"I say, padre," he barked, "for the past four years at these services you've announced the hymns and said the prayers and all that sort of thing, but I've never heard you preach. Why have you never preached for us?"

I explained that I found it very difficult to be the preacher on Battle of Britain Sunday because the Battle of Britain had taken place before I was born.

"Mmmmm. You're in trouble come Christmas" he said as he marched off towards the vol-au-vents.

My most vivid St Giles' memory is of the communion service for the General Assembly in 1969, when the Queen attended in person, and when her participation in the communion service introduced a much more practical problem than the ecclesiastical issues which I had raised in *The Glasgow Herald*.

In those days the Assembly met on a Tuesday, elected the moderator, did some business and then met early the next morning in St Giles' Cathedral for the Assembly communion service. The moderator that year was Dr Tom Murchison, a kindly Gael, who had followed the usual custom and chosen out of the elders attending the Assembly about twenty to serve communion in St Giles'. The Assembly office sent Harry Whitley a list of the elders taking part, and asked him to arrange for the customary rehearsal on the evening before the communion service. As arranged, Harry and I arrived at the cathedral and instantly he noticed that one of the elders was a woman. The eldership had been open to women for a number of years, and there was nothing improper in Dr Murchison including a woman in the list of elders he chose to serve at the communion. In the list sent to the minister of St Giles, she was referred to, quite accurately but unrevealingly as 'Dr McDonald'.

When Harry saw her he froze. His opposition to women elders (there were none in St Giles) and to women ministers (whom he would not allow in the pulpit) was legendary. I looked at the list of elders and their duties and realised that the elder assigned to give the communion cup to the Queen was Dr McDonald. Shortly afterwards this dawned on the minister of St Giles who said to me that this was a calculated insult to him, that by using the imprecise title 'Dr' he had been duped, that he would not attend the communion service the following morning, and would I now kindly drive him home.

Leaving the rehearsal in the hands of the session clerk of St Giles', I drove the minister home. He was in a very bad mood. I left him, saying that I would go home, phone the Principal Clerk of the General Assembly and talk to him about the difficulty which had arisen. "And make sure you tell him I won't be there tomorrow morning" Harry said as I left.

I still cannot believe that at the age of twenty seven, and ordained for only five months, I spent the next three hours on the phone to the Principal Clerk of the General Assembly, to officials of St Giles', to Michael Penney and Bertie Borland, two of Harry's closest friends and advisers in St Giles', and to the manse. Eventually about 10.30 in the evening I returned to the manse, where Harry, very, very reluctantly agreed that for the good of St Giles' he would turn up the following morning. It had been agreed that he would arrive only five minutes before the service started and that as soon as he had arrived we would process into the cathedral. Opportunities to dwell on the matter would be minimal. But as I left he said to me. "I'm only going through with this, Johnston, because you've promised me everything's going to be all right. But please, if I begin to say something I shouldn't, please, stay close beside me and stamp on my foot."

The next morning I picked Harry up and we drove into the cathedral. He was very subdued. We went into the vestry and Harry exchanged less than warm pleasantries with the moderator and his chaplains. I made some pathetic attempts at small talk and we got into line to process into the cathedral when the moderator's senior chaplain, another Gael who was not blessed with tact, turned to Harry and said "Harry, I hope you don't feel at all offended about this business of a woman serving communion to the Queen ..." He got not further when the minister of St Giles unleashed a not terribly controlled explosion. "Yes, I do object. I was offended. I think I have been treated quite shabbily, and ... and ... and... and you can take your foot off my toe, Johnston, because I'm going to say what I think ..." Fortunately the beadle caught my eye and moved the procession off very quickly!

I had been asked to stay at St Giles' for three years, but as my third year ended in 1970 Harry told me that he intended to retire in 1972, and asked me if I would be willing to stay on for a further year, until towards the end of 1971. David Ogston had established himself as an excellent assistant, and, Harry said, if I stayed for this extra year, David could then take over as senior assistant and he would see him through till his retiral.

By 1971 Heather was expecting our first child. We went for a short holiday to Ballater in February, and while we were there I got a message to say that Harry had suffered a stroke. We immediately returned to Edinburgh. He was in a nursing home, and the prognosis was good. He was expected to make a good recovery, but not in time to preach at a service, to be broadcast on radio throughout the UK, one of a series from cathedrals on "Difficult sayings of Jesus". When I visited Harry in the nursing home, he insisted that I tell the BBC that I was to preach at this service. Since he also insisted that he had just enjoyed a meal of pheasant pate, roast duck and roast potatoes and trifle, washed down with a half bottle of Chablis and a half bottle of Beaujolais, I did not take the instruction about preaching at the broadcast very seriously, When I phoned the BBC to say that Harry would not be able to preach, the producer, Douglas Aitken, with whom I was to work very frequently in the years ahead, and whom I was to succeed as Senior Producer in Religious Broadcasting, said, in his laid back way: "I suppose you'd better do it, Johnston".

And so I was introduced to the first of what was eventually to be very many services I conducted on radio. But nothing can erase the sheer terror of that first occasion. I remember very little about the broadcast, but I can remember, very, very clearly, processing into the cathedral that Sunday morning, and sensing goodwill and support from everyone.

Towards the end of 1971 a letter had arrived from the editor of *The Glasgow Herald* regretfully telling me that because of financial cutbacks he was having to dispense with some specialist correspondents and the Churches Correspondent was one of them.

In the summer of that year, I applied for the vacant church of Bellahouston Steven in Glasgow, and at the beginning of September, I was asked to preach as sole nominee, and was elected. The morning after I agreed to be sole nominee for

Bellahouston Steven, the interim moderator of a vacant church in Edinburgh phoned me, to say the this congregation's vacancy committee would like to hear me preach. I asked him to thank the committee for its interest, but to tell them that I had just agreed to be sole nominee for a church in Glasgow.

"You're quite right" he said. "It's always best to spend some time in the west before you come back to Edinburgh"!

3

I had lived for the first twenty three years of my life in Glasgow, but I literally only knew the half of it. The River Clyde does not only run through the centre of the city; it divides two quite different parts of it, the north from the south. I think in the years before I left home I very rarely crossed the river to the south side of the city. People from that side very rarely needed to, unless to visit friends, because, of course, the city centre was geographically on the north side. Most offices and shops were there. So the Ibrox district of Glasgow, where the parish of Bellahouston Steven was located, was an area I hardly knew at all. I dimly knew that in the thirties there had been a big exhibition in Bellahouston Park. I remembered, as a student, being sent to take pulpit supply in inaccessible Ayrshire villages, when I had travelled along Paisley Road West on a double-decker red bus, taking an hour and a half to get to places like Glengarnock and Dalry, but that was virtually my only contact with Glasgow south of the river.

I was very quickly to learn, however, that the part of Glasgow where I was to spend the next eight years was one of a number of quite distinct "villages" within the city. Many of the Ibrox people had been born into families which had spent generations in the area. Extended and inter-related families had formed a close-knit community for many years. But all this was about to change.

The M8 motorway which would sweep across the Clyde on the Kingston Bridge was to cut a huge swathe through the area and destroy the community. For nearly four years the church building would be, depending on the weather, the centre of a dust-bowl or surrounded by thick mud. One of the buildings the M8 was to devour was a red sandstone building in Gower

Street: Steven Memorial Church. Its congregation was of a reasonable size but mainly drawn from many of the tenements, of Clifford Street, Gower Street, and Scotland Street, which were to disappear along with the occupants' much loved parish church. The presbytery proposed a union between Steven Memorial and the neighbouring parish of Bellahouston, whose members lived either in the big villas of Dumbreck or in the low density tenements of Bellahouston Drive or the Halfway end of Paisley Road West. The compensation which Glasgow Corporation, as it then was, would give to the united congregation of Bellahouston Steven would provide a custom-built, brand new suite of halls which, the congregation had been promised, would be the envy of everyone in the south side of the city.

The two congregations, although very different in composition and background, had had tolerably good relationships until they were merged, a year or so before I became the minister. Whereas Steven Memorial was a typically down to earth Glasgow congregation, Bellahouston was, well, Bellahouston. From 1927 until the mid 1950s the minister was an Irishman of considerable social pretensions, who used to walk to church every Sunday in frock coat and tall tile hat. One of the kirk session in my day, a retired accountant, used to enjoy telling me how, as a small boy, he and his friends had once knocked the tile hat from the minister's head with a well-aimed snowball. Another long-standing office-bearer described to me a revealing exchange between an elder and the minister towards the close of his ministry. The elder explained that his minister had to understand that Bellahouston was gradually becoming a working class parish. "Over my dead body" he replied.

I once made what turned out to be the social gaffe of visiting a very elderly lady in one of Dumbreck's finer mansions about half past three in the afternoon. As she sat me down, this old lady looked at my sports jacket and grey trousers and informed me that Mr Coulter always wore a frock coat when he came to visit, and he would never have dreamed of calling at a house in Dumbreck in the afternoon. In the afternoon he visited on the other side of Paisley Road West and in the evening he dined in Dumbreck. "Well, you see, these were the days when ministers were gentlemen" I said, flippantly hoping to move the conversation on. "Oh no, Mr McKay, those were the days when ministers were ministers"!

Bellahouston, which was built in 1863, was twenty years older than Steven Memorial, which was built as a memorial to a notable churchman, Moses Steven, who had gifted the site for Bellahouston Parish Church. But Moses Steven was about all the two congregations had in common. The people of Steven Memorial, probably with some justification, felt slightly patronised by their neighbours, quarter of a mile away. One of the members who came from Steven Memorial explained the difference between the two congregations like this. "We in Steven Memorial had to do everything in the church ourselves. In Bellahouston they got three estimates and hired a tradesman."

However, the compulsory purchase of the Steven Memorial building led to a union between the two congregations in 1969, under the ministry of the Revd Walter Moffat, who, two years later, left a bitterly divided congregation for a parish in his native Ayrshire, and I succeeded him in November 1971.

I soon realised I faced three challenges.

The first was the immediate demolition of a large part of the parish, and with it the likelihood that a considerable number of members of the congregation would be leaving the area and would rightly join a congregation nearer their new home. I had inherited from my father a conviction that whatever else a minister might find to do with his time, his first priority after the preparation of worship was the regular, systematic visiting of the congregation. So shortly after the Christmas season

I told the congregation that I would be starting visiting the congregation, and I decided to begin with those homes which were due for demolition. It was very sad to hear stories from elderly people suddenly having to face being up-rooted after a lifetime in the Ibrox community. It was especially sad to see the disappearance, in the early stages of the demolition, of what had been an innovative piece of social policy on the part of Glasgow Corporation. Gower Square, as it was officially known, or "the old folks' flats" as everyone called them, housed something like a hundred and twenty single old people on three floors of small flats, built in a square, with connecting corridors open to the elements and overlooking a central grassed area. It had been effectively an experiment in sheltered housing without any warden system, because the flats were designed in such a way that most people were able to see a large number of their neighbours, and most were at the age where it was difficult to distinguish neighbourly concern from nosiness! But the important thing about Gower Square was that everyone did keep an eye open for other people. I was regularly telephoned by one resident to ask if I knew how another was because she hadn't been seen for quite some time. However Gower Square, and a lot more property, was demolished in order that, as I used to put it "we can all get to Greenock twenty minutes earlier than before, and if you've been to Greenock, you'll know that's a doubtful pleasure" (By this time my father had moved to be minister of a church in the west end of Greenock).

I cannot deny that it was demoralising for a young minister to watch his congregation decline, because of the number who moved away from the area, and more than once in my first year I went home wondering how on earth I was going to last out the five years that church rules required me to stay in my first parish. That demoralised feeling was not helped when I realised the extent of the second challenge: the bitter divisions within the congregation which seemed united in name only.

When the presbytery brokered the union between the two congregations, its basis and plan of union dealt with the legal necessities: which building would be used, and who would be the minister. (The minister of Steven Memorial had moved to another charge in Glasgow just before the union negotiations began). For obvious reasons, Bellahouston's building and minister had to be chosen. It was the session clerk and the Clerk to the Congregational Board from the former Bellahouston who continued in office in the united congregation. The more I learned, the more I had considerable sympathy for those from Steven Memorial who appeared to have lost out at every turn. However it was when the office-bearers of the two congregations planned the compromises that would need to be made to create a common practice that trouble had begun. It had been the practice in Bellahouston Parish for the elders to wear black morning coats at the communion services, whereas in Steven Memorial lounge suits were worn. In Steven Memorial the choir was robed but in Bellahouston it was not. The compromise which was reached was that in the united congregation elders would wear morning dress for communion, and the choir would wear robes. So virtually all the elders from Steven Memorial resigned *en bloc* and those formerly in the choir at Bellahouston refused to join the choir after the union took place. The result was that every Sunday the choir, made up mainly of former members of Steven Memorial, had to endure the angry glares of some of those who had been in the choir at Bellahouston, and I can vouch for the fact that the glares were fierce! On communion Sundays ordained elders, who had served in Steven Memorial for many years, sat in the pews, having resigned from the kirk session over the dress code.

There were some sources of division I could do very little about. The Woman's Guild in Bellahouston had done things one way; the Guild in Steven Memorial another. Older and wiser ministers than I had got into trouble for meddling in the politics of the Woman's Guild, especially on issues that were fundamental to the establishment of the Kingdom of God, such as the merging of two different patterns of Guild china, and deciding on what congregational occasions it might be appropriate for the Guild china to be brought out!

However there were some things I could try to do, and I was enormously helped when the session clerk, Ranald Macrae, decided to leave the area. He was a wise, good, man, who was devoted to the Church and to the congregation, but he belonged to Bellahouston. The opportunity arose to appoint a session clerk who would truly belong to the united congregation. I approached the man who had been senior elder in Steven Memorial, and who, virtually alone, had joined the kirk session after the union, and asked him who we should appoint. Without a moment's hesitation he said "Fraser Moffat", a wise and very witty man who had retired early from his post with the Electricity Board and lived barely fifty yards from the church.

Never was a young, inexperienced minister better helped by a session clerk. His patience with my impetuosity frequently diverted me from a course of action which he rightly saw spelled disaster. One afternoon I saw a light on in one of the church premises and went in to find Fraser engaged in some task or other. "I've had a letter from the local Orange Lodge" he said. "They'd like to hold a service in the church and have asked if you would preach". I exploded. "Fraser, you know I won't touch the Orange Lodge with a barge pole. And you know too that only the minister can give permission for a service to be held in the church and I'll never give my permission to the Orange Lodge. I can't abide what they stand for and I won't have it." I wanted to make myself clear! Fraser smiled but didn't say anything for a moment or two. "What on earth are you smiling at?" I asked him. "You're right, Johnston, and I knew that was what you'd say. But you'd be better to wait till you've been here longer before you talk like that about the Orange Lodge. So I told them the church was going to be redecorated and we wouldn't be able to let them have the service"!

Although Fraser had been a member of Bellahouston most of his days, and liked what he described as "dignity" in worship, he regretted the bitterness within the congregation, and did his very best to counteract it. He was very responsive when I suggested to him that I thought that the only way to resolve some of the tensions was to unpick the arrangements, made at the time of the union, which had led to resignations. If the kirk session decided to abandon the wearing of morning coats at communion, might the former Steven Memorial elders join the united session? And might a proposal that the choir leave their robes behind on a Sunday morning encourage others to join, and, perhaps, put an end to the pursed lips and steely glares which were aimed at the choir stalls every Sunday morning?

We agreed on the strategy, and it achieved what we wanted, though there were some on both sides who continued to mourn the passing of practices held dear.

There were other, more positive steps, which it was possible to take to try to overcome the past. Since the membership was dropping, because of shifts in the population, the congregation's income was in danger of dropping too. It seemed the right time to suggest that the congregation combine to hold autumn or Christmas Fairs, which, as well as raising income, might prove, as my former colleague at St Giles' David Ogston liked to put it that "the church that sweats together, gets together." I proposed to one of the former Bellahouston stalwarts, Anne Macalpine, who lived opposite the manse, that she might like to rent an empty shop in Paisley Road West and for a week run a sale of nearly new clothes. Anne spent almost all her spare time in charitable activity, but she embraced this one with such enthusiasm, and recruited helpers from the whole congregation with the result that (what for those days was) a huge amount of money was raised, and the strong-willed women from the two traditions in the congregation began to get to know each other through working together.

It was, however, a long haul and I must not give the impression that results were either immediate or even very permanent. One meeting, I think of the Congregational Board, long after these various attempts to heal divisions had been made, was particularly dreadful. A very acrimonious discussion broke out. It was quite clear that there were still unresolved resentments which were going to cause friction. I decided that the following Sunday I was going to tackle all this hostility and bitterness head on. I talked about reconciliation being at the heart of the Christian message. I told the congregation how one of my teachers at Cambridge, a theologian and archaeologist, had made a lifetime study of Christianity in North Africa, which had once been the focus and pride of Christian civilisation. Now, if he wanted to find any evidence of there ever having been a Christian church in North Africa, he had to dig deep down into the sand to excavate it, because all traces of Christianity had been virtually wiped out there; once, fifteen hundred years ago, a young man had sought out one of these Christian communities, along the North Africa coast, but had found it so riddled with bitterness, and severed by divisions, that he vowed never to have anything to do with the Christian faith again. The young man's name was Mohammed.

My sermon, I thought, had not missed and hit the wall! However, as I shook hands at the door of the church I saw the woman I regarded as the worst of the trouble-makers approaching me. I was preparing what I was going to say when she greeted me with a broad smile. "Well, I hope *they* all take it to heart".

The third challenge we faced was the building of the new halls which the compulsory purchase of the Steven Memorial Church building was to provide. A month or so after I was inducted, along with some office-bearers, I had a meeting with the architect, who had been appointed not by the congregation but by some agency of the presbytery. It was quite clear that the plans were going to cost more than the funds made available through compulsory purchase. It was clear that the office-bearer responsible for fabric was extremely capable at organising and completing the day-to-day property problems which church buildings presented. However, it was also clear he was far from able to handle delicate discussions with an architect who knew that, however unhappy the representatives of the congregation were with the cost of the plans he drew up, he had the ear of those in the presbytery who had negotiated the compulsory purchase and agreed on the building of the new halls. I searched the presbytery minutes diligently to find some reference to the work undertaken at Bellahouston Steven, but could find none.

Shortly before I arrived at Bellahouston Steven, an elder who had spent some years working south of the border, Jack Cumming, returned to the district and congregation. He had taken little part in the discussions about the new halls because when the union had been agreed he was not a member of the congregation. He was a civil engineer, and he began to be unhappy about what was being reported to kirk session and Congregational Board. He concluded that any plan to build new halls for the money provided by compulsory purchase was out of the question, and that the repeatedly revised plans by the architect were costing money and taking time. He advised the Congregational Board to dispense with the services of the architect, which it did, and ask another architect to draw up plans for an extension to the existing halls, with the understanding that there was an immutable ceiling on the cost of work and fees.

The upgrading of the existing halls and the extension, which comprised a large games hall, a series of rooms and an area linking all the halls to the church building, were opened in November 1975 and dedicated by the Very Revd Andrew Herron. The question which was then arising in my mind was – to what use were these buildings to be put? Were they just to make life for the congregation's own organisations more comfortable, or could they help towards restoring something of the sense of community which the coming of the M8 had caused?

I asked the kirk session to sponsor a project under the Job Creation scheme, to employ two community workers to undertake a survey of the area and report to the kirk session on what we could provide which the community felt it lacked. After some time the report concluded that at that time (1976) there were three forms of service to the community which the church could undertake. Those who lived around the area where the church stood were midway between two public libraries, both of which were considerable distance away and required public transport to visit. The provision of some form of library would be valued. Apart from traditional youth organisations, there was no unstructured youth club for young people in the area, many of whom roamed streets in the evenings and found trouble easily. A third need had been imported into the community. With the seizure of power in Uganda in 1972 by Idi Amin, and his subsequent expulsion of Asians who lived there, refugees had been housed first at a reception centre, created in a redundant primary school, and then in homes within the parish area. Their children were attending the local school, but their education was being hindered because the English language in which they were taught was not spoken in their homes. Nobody was providing teaching in English for the Ugandan Asians who had recently come into the area.

We extended the contracts of the community workers and set about meeting these three needs. The library presented no difficulty. That was the sort of obvious, understandable, sanitised sort of service which everyone in the church applauded and contributed to, both in time as voluntary librarians, and in the provision of books. It was immediately extremely popular, and continued to be so. Officially, local councillors and officials of the library service disapproved of our initiative, but privately we were asked to keep a close record of the number of people who borrowed books and of books borrowed, for there had been a plan to build a library just across Paisley Road West from the church. A site had been earmarked for years but in every round of cutbacks, the proposed Ibrox library was the first project to be ditched. I am pleased, and not a little proud, that shortly after I left Bellahouston Steven, the building of the new local library was begun. Our library and the statistics it provided had proved how much it was needed.

The provision of the youth club caused more controversy, as youth clubs on church premises frequently did. The existing uniformed organisations, particularly the Boys' Brigade, found that accommodation for activities – which had been assumed would be always available as of right – was in much more demand than, for example, the BB leaders had expected. The argument was regularly advanced at the kirk session that the Boys' Brigade was an organisation committed to the advancement of Christ's kingdom and as such should be given priority. I was extremely unpopular with the BB officers because, despite the fact that I had been in the Boys' Brigade myself, I refused to endorse this view. Occasionally, and not always very tactfully I must confess, I pointed out that in the years I had been minister, the Boys' Brigade had provided only one member for the church, and that I felt a project which met a need simply because it existed, without expecting any return in terms of involvement with the church was possibly more honest, and maybe even more Christian, than running an organisation which paid lip-service to a church commitment but did not succeed in promoting it.

I was probably influenced by a very unhappy experience early in my ministry at Bellahouston Steven. I accepted an invitation to spend a couple of days with the Boys' Brigade at their summer camp in Argyll. I was pretty horrified after the evening meal to be told by one of the officers that there was an "understanding" that the officers would go to one local pub and the boys would go to another, and so long as there was no encounter between them, then nothing openly need be said. When officers and boys gathered at the end of the evening for prayers, I was aware that one of the boys, well under age, was being shielded by others, but not sufficiently well to prevent me realising that he was very drunk. The following morning he looked extremely ill and wanted no breakfast. I was helping with the cooking, however, and piled a plate high with more greasy food than was good for him. "I don't want any left" I said as I put the plate in front of him. He knew, and I knew, and nothing else was said. Yet much more ought to have been said. I think I should have said more than to the Boys' Brigade captain than that I would not be returning again to his summer camp because I had not been impressed.

The wider membership of the congregation was unhappy that their new halls were sometimes treated by the kids who came to the youth club with less than the respect which they should, and there were frequent complaints about toilets being left in a mess, or graffiti on the walls, or scratches on the parquet flooring. I seem to remember preaching a lot of sermons which contained frequent references to statements like the famous one of the wartime Archbishop of Canterbury, William Temple, who said that the church is the only organisation that exists for the sake of those who are not members of it, or exploring themes like seeds growing secretly in the ground, or risking life in order to find it. More and more I began to reflect on how, like the small Christian communities to whom the apostle Paul wrote his letters, we were having to test what whether we really believed what we said we did against what we felt called to do as a Christian community.

There was most misunderstanding over the classes we started

to run to teach English to immigrants who had come to live nearby. Each case of the congregation's halls being used for community ventures had to be approved by the Congregational Board, a body made up partly of representatives of the kirk session and members elected by a congregational meeting. When the project came up for discussion at the Congregational Board I was afraid it might be a step too far for some.

One officebearer made a lengthy speech in which he said he was puzzled, confused and really quite surprised that I was suggesting providing for these Ugandan Asian immigrants. Didn't I know that they were all Moslems, and that there was no likelihood that any of them would become members of the church? So why were we bothering to run these classes? Then one of the younger elders, who was never afraid to speak out, and was known not to be very sympathetic to immigrants, got up to speak. I was anxious about what he was going to say. "Everybody knows my views" he began. "Everybody knows I would much rather these people weren't here. But if they're going to be here I think we'd better educate them". It was hardly a ringing endorsement of the diversity which flourishes in a multicultural society, but it was one big step for him, and it was enough to secure support for the project.

As the involvement with the community increased, my anxieties about how I was going to survive the first five years dissipated. When approaches from vacant congregations began, as the time when I was free to move passed, I found I had no wish to move. I got a lot of fulfilment from reaching out beyond the church doors, particularly from the chaplaincy at Summerston School, a school for those with physical and mental difficulties, which for several years operated in the parish of Bellahouston Steven. I became very interested in the school, and in how best to talk about faith and God to that particular group of children. Each week I took an Assembly and found the sort of bland things I might have said at a school assembly elsewhere impossible to deliver at this particular school's weekly assembly. As my involvement with the school grew, I became involved in a local authority education department working party, preparing a syllabus for religious education for this particular group.

It was tempting, but always a mistake, to assume that because of the difficulties these children faced they were somehow immune from natural youthful wickedness. Some of them knew only too well how to put their disability to effective use. There was one pupil, Ricky, who had lost both arms and a leg when he fell, from a railway bridge where he was looking for birds' eggs, onto electric railway cables. I first heard his story when he was in his early years of secondary school, and every year, whatever topic he was given for an English essay, always a variation on a similar theme like "A day I will never forget" or "The most important day in my life" he was able to turn to a description of the day he lost his limbs, and he had perfected the telling of the story, tapping out letters with a pencil held in his mouth on an electronic typewriter, so that no-one could read what he wrote without a tear in the eye, or failing to give it the highest possible mark. I was in the school, helping with the supervision of the leaving certificate examinations on the day Ricky was sitting his English O grade exam. When I glanced at the exam paper I realised that, yet again, Ricky was being given the opportunity, which of course he readily took, to tell his story word for word once more. I suspect when he sat Higher English he did so again, though I hope, for his sake, that he was given a different examiner!

Other pupils with poor eyesight were quite properly given twice the time given to pupils in other schools to complete their exams because they took a considerable length of time to read, particularly the exam papers which ran to several pages, and, of course, much, much longer to write their answers. But the physical exhaustion which set in often affected them considerably, and they were unable to give of their best.

Two things about Summerston School made me sad. The first was what I thought to be the insensitivity of including in the same special school, those with physical and mental disabilities. Far too often I thought the intellectual limitations of those with mental disability encouraged those with physical disabilities to assume that, as one of the physically disabled children said to me, "You shouldn't expect any of us here to pass examinations."

The other irony was that Summerston was a school which sat just across the road from Ibrox Park – home of Rangers' Football Club, which at that time had a quite clear policy of not signing any Roman Catholic players – but it was a school which took pupils from both Roman Catholic and Protestant homes. The even greater irony was that it took mental or physical disability to achieve a school where children were not segregated on religious grounds.

Rangers Football Club sent all the local Church of Scotland ministers free season tickets for seats at matches at Ibrox. Although I would have enjoyed spending Saturday afternoon watching football (when I was in Edinburgh, Harry Whitley and I spent most Saturday afternoons, when there was no wedding at St Giles, at Easter Road) I felt that if I was as critical as I was of Rangers' sectarian policy, it would be hypocritical to accept the club's hospitality.

In fact it was not Rangers' sectarianism which brought me into public conflict with the club, but a proposal for of all things, a carol service.

In 1976, Christmas Day fell on a Saturday, and the fixture list for the year showed that on Christmas Day Rangers and Motherwell were due to play at Ibrox. Rangers announced, at the end of September, that in order to give people the opportunity to be with their families, the match would be played on Boxing Day, a Sunday, and that it had invited the well-known Rangers supporter and populist minister the Revd James

Currie to conduct a carol service before the match. Along with a neighbouring minister, Revd Bob Bone, I publicly criticised both Rangers and Mr Currie. Our objections were not based on any sabbatarian views, which neither of us held. The presbytery of Glasgow, not long before this issue arose, had accepted a report from its Church and Community committee opposing Sunday football matches on the grounds of the disruption it caused to communities living close to Ibrox. Many people spent Christmas Day on their own, but visited families on Boxing Day, and we knew from our congregations the disruption which the influx of traffic into the area for a match on Boxing Day would cause. We felt that Rangers' statement that the match was to be played on Boxing day "to give people the opportunity to be with their families on Christmas Day" was just another way of saying that Rangers feared that the attendance on the scheduled day for the match would be low and the takings small. We also regretted that James Currie had agreed to "conduct" a carol service without consulting either the local ministers or the presbytery whose stated policy he was ignoring. But most of all we could not understand at all why, if the match had to be postponed, it could not have been postponed until Monday December 27th, which in most diaries was actually described as Boxing Day!

We were supported in our opposition to the match by the Convener of Strathclyde Region's highways and transportation committee. A fruitless meeting between representatives of Rangers and the presbytery was held, which was memorable only for the statement made by the Rangers' manager, Willie Waddell, "I'm as good a Christian as anyone; I never miss Songs of Praise on a Sunday"!

If I was deriving considerable satisfaction from involvement with the community outside the walls of the church, inside them, there was still a sizeable – although smaller than when I arrived – congregation Sunday by Sunday, which seemed to appreciate the services, and was extremely loyal. One very wet Sunday morning in February, when the rain lashed against the vestry window, I reckoned there would be few worshippers. Fraser Moffat, the session clerk, put his head round the door. "It's the sort of dreadful morning when only the aged and infirm will be able to get out" he said, with prophetic accuracy!

I think that the attendances on Sunday mornings owed something to visiting the congregation district by district, and getting round most of the six hundred or so in the course of a year. It is a practice which, even then, thirty years ago, was already regarded as antediluvian. I remember being asked by Murdo Ewen Macdonald, when he was Professor of Practical Theology at Glasgow University, to give a talk to divinity students about regular congregational visiting, because it was something they would not hear about from anyone else, he said. He clearly regarded how I spent a lot of my time as quite old-fashioned. I found my way into Murdo Ewen's own lectures for an incident which occurred one Sunday when he came to preach. He told me shortly after I was inducted that if he was free he would be happy to come to preach any time I asked him, on two conditions: that he got no fee, and that he did not have to give a talk to the children.

So on this Sunday morning I was talking to the children. I had been going through the letters of the alphabet, one a week, and after asking the children what words began with the letter of the week, I talked for a few moments about a word I had in mind. The previous Sunday I had asked the children if they could tell me words which began with the letter "u" and the (then) five- or six-year old daughter of an up-and-coming surgeon told me that "uterus" began with the letter "u". Though accurate, I did not find this helpful and quickly moved on to my moral for the day. Knowing that the girl would be there the following Sunday, and that the letter "v" provided further opportunities for her to share her medical vocabulary with me,

I decided on a more directive approach. Instead of asking the children for words beginning with "v" I asked them the name of the room which was behind the door on the other wide of the church, where I got ready for church. There was very little response. Eventually after some quite long silences and a few inaccurate suggestions, a Sunday School teacher came to my rescue and told the little boy sitting next to her to shout out the word "vestry", which she did. At which our second son Robert, by then aged three, yelled out "That's where daddy does a wee-wee before the church". Collapse of congregation, and hysterical laughter from Murdo Ewen in the pulpit, who began his sermon by telling the congregation that he now had the perfect example to include in his lectures of what to avoid in preparing a children's talk!

As I grew in experience, and I hope maturity, as a minister in Bellahouston Steven, I found myself reflecting more on two things: one an issue of practical theology, the other an incident which for me was pivotal in my development.

The issue which concerned me was the extent to which the shape which the congregation's outreach took, and the work which it undertook, and the focus which it gave to its Christian commitment would become permanent features of the congregation's attitude, or simply reflections of the sort of leadership which I was providing. In other words, I wondered whether, if there were important things we were learning together about what it meant to be a Christian community in this area of Glasgow, they were lessons which would remain if the time came when I moved on somewhere else.

At the time this was something which I thought about quite a lot, without ever resolving in my mind the issues it raises for leadership within the Christian community. Since then I have left not only Bellahouston Steven, but Paisley Abbey to which I moved in 1978, and in both places have been succeeded by ministers whose emphasis has been very different, and in many ways at odds with mine That is not to imply that my emphasis was automatically right and my successors' has been of necessity wrong. Far from it. It is, however, to raise questions about the nature of Christian leadership in a local community where the leadership is temporary and transient.

One approach to the issue would be to question whether leadership is what the ordained ministry in a local situation should be providing, and to suggest that the model of the enabler or the facilitator is a much more appropriate one for the ordained ministry. I understand that view and at the time I thought it profoundly mistaken. I believed that local congregations only thrive where they can look to and expect real leadership from the minister. I still have a lot of sympathy with that view, but I cannot entirely go along with it now. As I will explain, I am less convinced that a ministry ordained so that it, and it alone, can perform certain sacramental actions continues to be justified. But even were it to be justified, I suspect the organic relationship between minister and congregation lives only for the time in which it exists and it only has reality while the relationship does exist. What was right and real at the time is right and real for that time, and has no more relevance when the minister moves on than it could have relevance to the period before he or she arrived.

The incident which more than any other rocked me back on my heels was the suicide of a bright, attractive young woman in the congregation. She was a single mother, but she seemed more than capable of handling the problems that involved, because her sister lived nearby and regularly helped with childminding, and her father lived very close too.

One afternoon I got a phone call to say that this bright young mother had committed suicide. Immediately I went to her father's house. I had paid pastoral visits there before but they had never ventured beyond the politely social.

When he opened the door and recognised me his face turned very angry.

"What the hell do you want?"

I explained that I had heard what had happened to his daughter, and said that I had come to see if there was anything I could do to help, and might I come in?

"You're not crossing this door because I don't want to hear what you're going to say"

I said I would go, but before I did, could he, perhaps, tell me what I was going to say that he didn't want to hear?

He became even more angry and told me that I was going to tell him that his daughter's death was God punishing him because he had not gone to church as often as he should.

I said, very quietly, that not only was I not going to say that but not for a moment did I believe it.

There was a pause. "You had better come in" he said.

The next morning I went with him, as he had asked me to do when I eventually left his house the previous evening, to identify his daughter's body and begin to make the funeral arrangements. I will forget the scenes in the mortuary long before I will forget the question in my mind then, and for the days leading up to the funeral, and for a long time afterwards: what was it in the life of the Christians he knew, or in the faith of the community where I was minister, which made that distraught father think that when I called I was going to tell him his daughter's death was God punishing him for failing to go to church?

Quietly I began to resolve that whatever else the future held for me, I would do everything I could to convey a very different picture of what Christians believed.

Years later that resolve was to be reinforced. I was a regular contributor to a little slot on Radio Scotland called *Prayer Desk* which was broadcast each evening just before the ten o' clock news. I got home from contributing my two minutes' worth to the programme when the phone rang.

A voice said "You don't know me and I can't even tell you where I live because I am too frightened I will be found out, but something you said this evening made me think that I could speak to you."

There was a silence when I waited for him to say more, but the silence went on so I asked "What do you want to talk to me about?"

"I'm a homosexual. I go to church every Sunday and when I leave I feel more guilty than I was. I need to know that it is all right for me to belong to the church, and something you said tonight made me feel I could talk to you".

I cannot remember what I said, nor does it matter. We talked for half an hour or so, and then the conversation ended. I felt very ashamed that Christian faith had so humiliated someone. Again, I promised myself I would do everything I could to convey a very different picture of what Christians believe and expect.

4

During my years in Bellahouston Steven, I spent a considerable amount of time on presbytery business. The presbytery clerk, Andrew Herron, introduced me to the work of what was then called "readjustment": the uniting or linking of congregations in areas where once there had been a strong church presence but where, due to shifts in population, it was no longer viable to maintain the number of congregations there once had been. I accompanied Andrew Herron to meetings with office-bearers, learned from him the art of persuading office-bearers to agree to a little at a time, and gradually became convinced that if the Church of Scotland was going to survive it simply had to reduce the amount of money it was spending on buildings which were quickly emptying.

Usually one evening a week I was out somewhere in the city, trying to persuade a set of office bearers that the church's future depended on them abandoning their building, or encouraging another set of office-bearers to welcome a nearby congregation which was likely to close. I became an enthusiastic member of the presbytery's, and then the General Assembly's, committee on Unions and Readjustments, and spent one year trying to persuade the presbytery committee to endorse a plan to reduce the number of congregations in Glasgow presbytery by half and to approve a plan for each area indicating which churches must close whenever the next vacancy arose. It was preposterously impractical, and incredibly naïve. And although I continued to be heavily involved in the work of readjustment when I left Glasgow for Paisley, I now believe the closure of congregations in the sixties, seventies and eighties to have done real harm to the cause of the Church of Scotland, and my zeal for the cause of readjustment to have been terribly mistaken. It was so short sighted, assuming that in areas where there had been depopulation there would be no future regeneration. This has proved to be quite wrong. I now drive through areas of Glasgow where, in the sixties and seventies, churches were closed, sold, or demolished because round them stood what Andrew Herron used famously to call "a sea of red blaize". In these areas there are now modern houses, new communities, and no churches! Of course, where motorways were going to take over the landscape there could be no future for churches, but so much of our planning in the sixties and seventies failed to foresee the huge building programme of the last decade of the twentieth century, which created communities of quite considerable size without any visible church presence close by.

It took me quite some time to realise that the arithmetic of church closure simply did not add up. Two congregations of five hundred members did not produce a congregation of one thousand. It usually produced a congregation of six hundred and fifty, and the remainder was lost entirely to the church. "Dead wood" was the answer I used to give, but in the long run, who gained by cutting the dead wood off from the possibility of being ignited?

I remember hearing an amusing story about an old minister who had occupied the same pulpit for over fifty years and was now well into his eighties. Members of the kirk session decided to broach with the minister the question of whether it might be time for him to consider retiring.

"And why should I retire?" the minister asked his office-bearers.

They replied that the congregation now had tremendous difficulty hearing what the minister was saying on a Sunday morning.

"And how would they hear me any better if I retired?" the old minister barked back!

I think I would now ask, in the spirit of that story, how

the church was served by reducing the number of buildings, if circumstances led a third of the membership unable to hear even the distant call of the Gospel.

In the cause of readjustment I once did have to persuade an old minister he should retire. He was, I recall, over eighty five. Every week another bit of his church building fell down, and his congregation had dwindled to around fifty. We met in Andrew Herron's office, and after outlining all the circumstances, I explained that the only way open was for this old minister to retire and allow his congregation, who recognised their building was beyond repair, to unite with another, only a few yards away.

"I always wanted to die in harness" the old minister said quietly.

"That's usually all very well for the horse but pretty awful for the harness," Andrew Herron commented.

The old minister agreed to retire, and I went along to the office-bearers of the neighbouring congregation to ask them to agree to a union with the congregation which now would have no minister and no building. I spoke about how Christian faith believed that new life could emerge from what was old, that Christian fellowship required a welcome to be given to those who were disappointed, and that Christian charity required perhaps a change of name, so that something of the old congregation which was finished could be brought into the new, united congregation.

I thought the speech had gone down quite well until one of the office-bearers fixed me with a glare as steely as the rivets he worked with in the shipyards.

"All very well you coming here and talking about Christianity" he said, "but it's the future of the Church we want to discuss"!

However, I think there is an argument, deeper than these practical ones, against the pragmatic policy of church closures. In the days when I supported it, I used to say at meetings that the Church isn't buildings, it's people; and that when the New Testament uses the word "church", it never means bricks and mortar but members. I used to argue that church buildings are notoriously uneconomic and absurdly impractical and grossly underused.

I now wonder whether that was the judgment of an age whose standards I had uncritically accepted, and which measured everything precisely and expected everything to be costed precisely.

Some years ago I made a radio programme with David Jenkins, then about to retire as Bishop of Durham. He was asked whether it mattered to him that so many churches in his diocese were hardly ever used, and when they were used they were virtually empty, and Jenkins said that it didn't concern him in the slightest. So long as there were some people keeping these churches going, he said, then these church buildings were beacons, lights, signals, signs, symbols for the world around that there was another dimension to life, even if most of the time the world around them seemed not to be interested.

When King's College Chapel in Cambridge was built, with its high, carved, vaulted roofs and its majestic pillars and stunning stained glass, it could seat around two thousand people, I suppose. But when it was built, King's College had just seventy two students. It was built on the massive scale, not because the authorities were expecting a sudden increase in student numbers, but because they were trying to reflect their worship of the glory of God. Reflecting something of the grandeur and mystery of God requires something more than the custom-built, prosaic and functional.

People need places which are more eloquent than words to welcome new life, and to hallow love, and to mourn death. They need places which will convey for them what the poet Philip Larkin described as "the hunger in ourselves to be more serious". And when they have found that, it is both futile and wrong for someone like the young minister I was, to come along and tell them blithely that these places should not matter because the church is about people and not buildings.

When the number of men and women who were prepared to become ministers of the church was declining, it was quite right to point out that there would have to be a reduction in the number of congregations with a minister. However if small groups of Christian people could keep going a much-loved building without a full-time or conventional ministry, then would the church not have been better advised to find ways of allowing that to happen instead of taking steps to close the building? At least those who claimed to belong to the Church of Scotland would have continued for rather longer than they did, when unions gave them an excuse to remove their names and their allegiance from the Kirk's membership.

All these cold, wet winter evenings, zealously spent in a cause I now regard as mistaken!

In 1973, I was invited to be part of a group which was planning to launch a presbytery newspaper, *The Bush*. *The Bush* was the brainchild of Andrew Herron, and the journalist Bill Black, and after a couple of years, I became joint editor along with the maverick minister of Partick Newton Place, Donald Macdonald, and then, when Donald left to join the BBC's Religious Broadcasting Department I took over as sole editor.

Andrew Herron was very clear what he thought the purpose of *The Bush* should be. He wrote in his volume of memoirs, *Minority Report*, that he envisaged "a monthly newspaper that would tell both of what had happened at the recent presbytery meeting and of what was currently afoot within the bounds."

As they say in Glasgow "haud me back"! The idea that a newspaper would sell on the basis of a monthly report on a presbytery meeting was hardly riveting; and when we started investigating, we found that very little, which merited the term news, was actually happening within the presbytery,. There were any number of kirk socials, whose conveners felt that anything less than two thousand words in the presbytery newspaper failed to do justice to the occasion, and plenty of interesting events about which the sponsors never quite got round to informing anyone. A number of bodies, most notably at the time Christian Aid, appeared to adopt the motto "silence is golden" towards any publicity that *The Bush* might give them.

So, when news was hard to come by within the church, we went to look for it, and so stories appeared about the infamous organisation "Children of God" which tried to recruit young girls to become involved in bars and strip clubs, so that, the sect said in one of its publications, "they could go through the same kind of sacrifices Jesus went through". One pamphlet, *Dirty Dishes,* answered one girl's question about why she "had to get so dirty to save them" like this. "You have to go down there and get dirty with their looks, and their caresses and their kisses, and even their own semen of hard loving that they might be clean".

This organisation was openly attempting to recruit girls in shopping centres and malls across the city, and in a front page exclusive which was followed up in broadsheets and tabloids, the cult's methods were described and parents warned of the danger.

A motion criticising me for carrying the story was proposed at the next presbytery meeting but was overwhelmingly rejected, though the proposer's complaint that I had given the sect unnecessary publicity seemed a little thin when, the morning after the presbytery meeting, the story of the attack on the Editor of *The Bush* was on radio news bulletins and in most newspapers!

And if news was difficult to come by, *The Bush* resorted, not too unwillingly, to publishing opinion. In order to reconcile editorial opinion with the presbytery's ownership of the newspaper, it was agreed that the masthead should be changed from the original "News and Views of Glasgow presbytery" to "News and Views *from* Glasgow presbytery". Probably no-one except a few critics noticed, or cared about, the change.

One editorial I wrote in support of a controversial book published in 1977, *The Myth of God Incarnate,* led to me being accused of heresy in the presbytery but the circulation of the newspaper continued to increase. No one, least of all myself, was deluded into imagining that because *The Bush's* much bigger secular cousins took up stories or quoted editorials, they were any the more important for that. But the attention which the national press paid to *The Bush* helped establish it in the mind of the church-going public, and that helped it to sell. Voices crying in the wilderness may be prophetic, but in circulation terms they are not profitable.

It is only fair to record that the policy which Donald Macdonald and I adopted – and I continued – was not one which Andrew Herron, the presbytery Clerk, agreed with. He flatteringly describes Donald Macdonald and me as "both men of outstanding skill, but both fired with the same ambition – to see our little paper recognised and quoted by the nationals." He continues "They considered that no issue had justified its existence unless a reference to it appeared, preferably on the front page, of the next day's newspaper. For myself I was most unhappy about this, and to this day I feel it marked the first step on our downward path. In my experience the appetite for sensation is an insatiable one, and you are wise not to try to satisfy it. Our objective had been to tell a very simple story about some of the kindly, gracious, generous things that are going on in the world, things too often unrecorded and unrecognised. Telling of the other things we were happy to leave to the tabloids. There was, we believed, news to be told about the way the Kirk was running at the congregational level, news that was worth hearing and that people would enjoy reading … As we gained headlines we lost readers, and with falling circulation we began to run into difficulty with advertising."

Andrew Herron was, of course, entitled to his opinion, but just a few months before I gave up the editorship, we reported a surplus of over £2000 for the year to the presbytery. This was spent on paying for an annual presbytery year book, for a professionally produced tape/slide presentation for use by the presbytery in promoting deeds of covenant, and the remainder was given to the presbytery's Lodging House Mission in the east end of Glasgow. At that time, despite Andrew Herron's comments about falling circulation, the circulation and the advertising was secured. It was precisely when *The Bush* became the extended parish magazine which Andrew Herron wanted it to be that circulation dropped, advertising revenue fell and the publication, sadly, was abandoned. I regularly tried to convince Andrew Herron of the old journalist's adage: "It's what they don't want printed that's news; all the rest is just publicity", but I failed.

As well as a commitment to taking part in the work of Glasgow presbytery, a sideline in broadcasting developed while I was minister of Bellahouston Steven.

I was asked, in 1972, to record five *"Thought for the Day"* programmes in connection with a week of events commemorating the death of John Knox. As I arrived at Broadcasting House in Glasgow, I was very nervous, but the producer, Father Bill Anderson, adopted a technique of coping with a contributor's nerves which I have found very useful myself. He told me that he wanted to make sure that each contribution was right for length, so would I just go into the studio, make myself comfortable, and read them through so that he could time them. Then we would record them. I relaxed and read the scripts through. "That's fine. Let's go for coffee" Father Bill said, putting his head round the studio door.

"No, I'd rather get the recording over first" I replied.

"I recorded you reading them through. They sound good!" And off we went for coffee.

The next time I was asked to contribute a week of thoughts was two years later, in February 1974, and they were no longer recorded. I had to go, early in the morning, to Broadcasting House and read my script live. The reason a change was made from recorded contributions to live ones lay in a recorded *Thought for the Day* in the summer of 1972. The contributor had recorded five talks, all linked to the Olympic Games which were then taking place. One morning he began with something like "Don't you just wish you could be in Munich for the Olympics" and went on in a very cheery vein for some time. Sadly eleven Israeli athletes had been murdered the previous day. So it was decided that *Thought for the Day* should be live.

My second invitation came at the last minute because in February 1974 the Prime Minister, Mr Heath, called a General Election. The contributor already booked to do *Thought for the Day* in the first week of the election campaign was considered to be a dangerous Marxist who could not be trusted to maintain the BBC's vital balance during an election campaign. That contributor, whose place I took as a more safe choice, was the young rector of St Ninian's Pollokshields, Richard Holloway!

I will have more to say about *Thought for the Day* when I come to deal with my years as a producer of the programme, but since those days I have been a regular contributor. I began to be invited first to take part and then either to write or to present other radio programmes, and in the mid-seventies I began a partnership with the legendary broadcaster Vernon Sproxton, presenting coverage on radio of the General Assembly of the Church of Scotland from then until 1987.

Vernon was a Yorkshireman, and a Congregationalist minister, who had had a very distinguished career as a maker of radio and television documentaries. His scripts were masterpieces of the writer's art, and he could convey an impression in phrases that he seemed to coin effortlessly. It was he who on one Assembly report suddenly described the procession of ex-moderators who rose to speak in a debate as "geriatric grenadiers". The phrase stuck. Part of the success of the chemistry of these programmes was in the apparent role reversal. The journalist Harry Reid, in *The Scotsman*, described Vernon as "very English, very smooth, very mellifluous, just a little oily. Johnston McKay, who presents Assembly reports with him sounds very Scottish; hard, spiky combative. Yet McKay....is the man who finds himself in the role of Establishment figure; he has to defend the Assembly, while Sproxton tilts at it..... Sproxton is the ideal man to prick self-importance, self-satisfaction, self-deceit, excessive legalism and bureaucratic pomp, all of which loom from time to time at the Assembly. What I find confusing about him is that all his barbs and digs are presented in such a fluent, almost unctuous manner.....The nightly commentary by Sproxton and McKay has sustained interest when reports on the Assembly could easily have been crushingly boring. As it was, the extracts from the Assembly cried out for their incisive comments."

Joyce Macmillan, then radio critic of *The Glasgow Herald* did little for our modesty by suggesting in a review of the Assembly programmes that Vernon and I should be transported to present "Today in Parliament"!

The invitation to take part in Radio Scotland's Assembly coverage was a very formative moment in my career. Even at the time I was aware that by agreeing to contribute, and describing and analysing exactly what I believed was happening, or by reporting what I had gathered about the way the Assembly was run, I was not likely to make the sort of friends in the church's corridors of power who would make me welcome there. However, if I made my comments in a way that the kirk establishment found unexceptional, or withheld information which might shed light on what was going on in the Assembly, I would not provide what was expected of me by the production team.

The dilemma was posed sharply during one General

Assembly when a minister's dismissal from his church had been confirmed by the Assembly's Judicial committee, which then sought the Assembly's approval: normally a formality. However when the minutes of the Judicial committee were published in the Assembly papers, it appeared that a number of people who were at the meeting had not had their attendance recorded, and a number who were not at the meeting had been listed as present. It appeared that because of the inaccuracies in the minute, the decision of the Judicial Commission would not be approved, and the future of the minister in question would be open to doubt.

I was told in conversation with someone involved in the proceedings that the reason the attendance record was so inaccurate was that the then Principal Clerk had used the back of the signed attendance sheet to send down to the restaurant in the church offices the list of what everyone wanted for lunch. Understandably the piece of paper had been thrown in the bin after the order was prepared, and the clerk made up the attendance from his clearly faulty memory. This was just one of a large number of glaring mistakes made by the then Principal Clerk, which everyone complained about, but nobody was prepared to bring out into the open. So, in the programme that night I used what I knew of the reason for the failure of the Church's judicial process to talk about the failings at the heart of the organisation which was responsible for running the General Assembly. I knew as I talked that if the door to the corridors of power was still slightly open, it would slam closed very quickly. I had made my choice.

However taking part in the Assembly coverage with Vernon Sproxton had far more significant effects on me.

Vernon was not just a consummate broadcaster. He was a totally committed *religious* broadcaster. By that I don't just mean that he made programmes about God, theology or the church. I mean that he regarded programme making as a vocation and constantly reflected on it in the light of his religious and theological convictions. From what I had seen of producers up until then, I had thought of programme-making as a very practical activity, which required judgment about presenters and contributors but was a somewhat mechanical process thereafter. Vernon taught me otherwise. Partly because we talked mostly when we were working together at the General Assembly, when the church expected to be able *to use* radio and television (and those of us who worked in the these media) for its own purposes, Vernon showed me that it is not possible properly to understand broadcasting unless you *respect* the broadcast media. He once wrote this about television, but it applies to radio as well:

"Respect for the medium means taking seriously the enormous potential of television, with its capacity for extending the range of our experience, the range of the eyes and the feet, exposing whole areas of life, opening new windows of comprehension, *transporting* people within the limits of your budget, and your resources, and your facilities and your time".

Just before I had met Vernon, I had become a member of the Scottish Religious Advisory committee of the BBC and through Ian Mackenzie, recently appointed Head of Religious Programme, had met producers he had brought in, who were far more concerned for religious broadcasting as Vernon Sproxton understood it than about relaying church services or conveying a "religious" message.

One television programme reflects the difference. It was called *Another Kirk*. The cameras spent an evening in a pub in Glasgow's Shettleston Road. The punters talked about God, religion, faith and the church. Most of what they said bore very little resemblance either to my own faith or to the faith of people I knew. A lot of what they said about the church was inaccurate and prejudiced. No sooner had the programme been transmitted than the Church was up in arms that such blatant misrepresentation should have been broadcast. Quite apart from the stunning camera work and brilliant direction, I found the programme riveting because it challenged two assumptions I had made, ever since I was a divinity student, that if reasonable explanations of what Christianity stood for could be got across, then people would recognise, as I did, that Christianity itself was reasonable; and that although church attendance was declining, there was a general understanding of and sympathy for what the church was about. However, here, within half an hour, I was being shown that although reasonable Christianity had been disseminated in popular paperbacks or radio and television programmes for quarter of a century, nothing had penetrated to those in the pub, who, far from being sympathetic to the church, were extremely sceptical of it. The one person who made an impact on them was a woman in Salvation Army uniform, who responded willingly to an invitation to sing *The Old Rugged Cross*.

I was more than disappointed that so many in the Church failed to see what this film might be saying *to them*, and could not see that the mistaken impressions and false descriptions which the programme conveyed were not just nonsense to be dismissed but signals to be interpreted. It was Vernon Sproxton, who taught me to "read" radio and television programmes properly.

He also introduced me to poetry. Or rather he "re-introduced" me, because, of course, I had been taught poetry at school. I remember in my sixth year English class, reading poems from Palgrave's *Golden Treasury* aloud in class, each in turn until our bored teacher would ask the next-in-line to take over. Every so often he would interrupt with a laconic comment. "Note the imagery, note the imagery" and then ask the reader to continue.

Every so often in the course of conversation, or during a broadcast, Vernon would throw in a line or two from poetry. I first heard the name of Edwin Muir from him when he quoted "the Word made flesh here is made word again". I recall him, in a discussion about something very mundane which the General Assembly had decided, suddenly quoting "here, among sordid particulars, the eternal design appears", or, on another occasion, saying of a speech which he had thought quite correct but insincere "It reminds you of Eliot, doesn't it? 'The last temptation is the greatest treason, to do the right thing for the wrong reason'".

I began to read poetry again, initially because I recognised that poets said things in such a powerful way that quoting from them made a point more powerfully than I could, but very soon I began to discover that the language of poetry was the most true way to communicate the Gospel. By that I do not just mean that so much of the bible is written in the language of poetry, though so many of the difficulties people have with Christian faith would disappear if they realised that. I mean that poets use words precisely, but they use them to hint at meanings which are often not clear and frequently ambiguous. I began to discover that the ambiguity of the poet's language is often a reflection of the ambiguity at the heart of what Jesus of Nazareth had to say and the way he said it. As the Danish teacher Kierkegaard put it: "You cannot tell people what to do" (or, I would add, what to believe) "you can only tell them parables, and that is what art really is, particular stories of particular people and experiences, from which each according to his immediate and particular needs may draw his conclusions".

Gradually my preaching changed from trying to explain what passages in the bible "actually meant", to exploring the hints, glimpses, signals, and signs that might be contained in them. I began to realise that a preaching style which attempted to resolve the ambiguities in faith or the contradictions in the message of Jesus was in fact distorting both faith and the Gospel. Jesus was ambiguous. He taught in parables, so he said, "so that they may see and not perceive, they may hear and not understand." He told stories which are capable of more than one interpretation, sometimes of contradictory interpretations, and the person who seeks for clarity always wants to resolve the ambiguities and iron out the paradoxes and reconcile the contradictions. But if the ambiguities and paradoxes and contradictions are of the very essence of Jesus' teaching (and not just his teaching method) then the person who seeks clarity is falsifying the teaching.

John Tinsley, who was Bishop of Bristol, wrote in an article in the journal *Theology*, "The human mind is ill at ease with ambiguity and paradox. This is especially the case with the religious mind, which has a special impetus to convert all ambiguities and paradoxes into the most explicit and unequivocal assertions, while remaining blind to the half-truths it creates in the process. We have paid a heavy price for the assumption that the model for the Christian preacher (and indeed teacher) is the Old Testament prophet with his 'Thus says the Lord'. No doubt the attraction of the model was that it seemed to give indubitable authority to the preacher or teacher. But it is possible to be authoritative without being authoritarian."

The title of the article from which that quote came is "Tell it slant", which in turn comes from a poem by Emily Dickinson:

"Tell all the truth but tell it slant –
Success in Circuit lies.
Too bright for our Infirm Delight
The Truth's superb surprise.
As lightning to the children eased
With explanations kind
The Truth must dazzle gradually
Or every man be blind."

Or, as the poet W.H. Auden put it
"Truth in any serious sense
Like Orthodoxy, is a reticence".
Poets do use words *precisely* but the language of poetry is *ambiguous*. And in that sense the language of Jesus is like the language of poetry, which always leaves room for the reader to breathe. As T.S. Eliot wrote
"What you do not know is the only thing you know
and what you own is what you do not own
and where you are is where you are not"
Or, as a Russian author said "I knew a man who saw God so clearly that he lost his faith".

5

As 1976 drew to a close, I had been approached by the vacancy committees of two congregations, asking if I would be interested in being considered as their minister. I had not applied for either, and, before the approaches from them, I had not intended to consider a move. However, as often happens, the approaches made me unsettled, and after discussing things with my wife Heather, we decided that if either of these congregations got round to asking me to be their minister, I would accept.

The two congregations concerned were Dumbarton Riverside and Paisley Abbey, and in the event it was the Abbey's vacancy committee which invited me to be their sole nominee. When, a couple of days after getting the invitation to become minister there, I phoned the interim moderator of Dumbarton Riverside to ask him to tell the vacancy committee there that I was no longer available, he told me that the vacancy committee would be very upset because it had decided late the previous evening to invite me. He told me that the committee now had no other serious candidates and asked if I could suggest anyone. As it happened, I knew my friend Jim Miller, then in Peterhead, was interested in a move. The vacancy committee heard him the following Sunday and immediately asked him to be sole nominee. Our two inductions, in Dumbarton and Paisley, had to be arranged so each of us could be present at that of the other.

It took me some time to piece together the not entirely creditable story of how I came to be minister of Paisley Abbey. The congregation had been vacant since June 1976, when the minister, James Ross, died. By January 1977 the vacancy committee was divided equally between two ministers – let's call them Mr Smith and Mr Brown – and the committee had a preference for Mr Smith. Then the vacancy committee got a letter from a senior churchman, indicating that he knew the dilemma that the committee faced, but that he felt obliged to point out that Mr Smith was a "promiscuous homosexual" and were he to be invited to become minister of Paisley Abbey, this churchman would make this information public. Some of the vacancy committee decided that the letter should be ignored, but the majority felt that it should be heeded. There was not a sufficient majority at the time for the other candidate, Mr Brown, and it was decided that the committee should take another look at the potential field.

That is when I came into the picture, and eventually the committee, without dissent, agreed to invite me rather than Mr Brown. To complicate the picture, Mr Brown was also a candidate for Dumbarton Riverside, and he made the fatal mistake of contacting the Paisley Abbey committee and telling them that he had been asked to be minister of Dumbarton Riverside, and that unless Paisley Abbey asked him within a couple of days he would accept the Dumbarton invitation, which, of course, he had not received!

Paisley Abbey stands right in the centre of the town, surrounded by roads. Parts of it date back to the twelfth and thirteenth centuries, but by far the most imposing part of the Abbey, the choir, was restored to its present condition only in 1929. Adjoining the Abbey are a number of old monastic buildings called the Place (Palace) of Paisley, including a minister's residence which was restored largely due to the energy and drive of the minister of the Abbey from 1950 to 1969, the Revd Dr William Rogan. As soon as it was announced that I was to be the minister of Paisley Abbey, I received a long letter from Dr Rogan, urging me to live in the residence within the Place of Paisley. My wife and I had been shown round it by the then session clerk, Alex Leishman, who assured me that the benefits of living in a house without having to pay a penny for heating and lighting were considerable.

We were less than convinced. Our two boys, Kevin and Robert, were, then, aged eight and five, and would have had to be taken everywhere because of the traffic surrounding the Abbey. They would also have been isolated from any friends they might make. I was also unconvinced that the benefits of free heat and light outweighed the disadvantage of having no privacy whatsoever, since only a short staircase separated the entrance to the minister's residence from the rooms where committees and organisations met. My predecessor James Ross and his family had lived in the minister's residence, and he suffered his fatal heart attack there. I was not sure whether illness and location were unconnected.

Normally a minister going to a new congregation would have little or no say in where he stayed. That there was a choice open to me was owing to the man I had crossed swords with from time to time in Glasgow presbytery, Dr Andrew Herron. When Dr William Rogan had completed the restoration of the minister's residence within the Place of Paisley, he approached the presbytery of Paisley to have it designated as the manse of Paisley Abbey. Andrew Herron was then Clerk of Paisley presbytery. Convinced of its unsuitability as a manse, he convinced the presbytery not to designate Dr Rogan's restored house as the manse, but rather as "the minister's residence", and persuaded the presbytery to go further and insist that any future minister of Paisley Abbey should be offered the option of living elsewhere. When I told him I was moving to Paisley, Andrew Herron mentioned the residence and said, in a typically pawky way that "if you bang your head on a low beam, it's no comfort to know that it's a sixteenth century beam".

When I had been asked by the vacancy committee if I would be prepared to live in the minister's residence, I indicated that if and when I was elected minister I would consider that problem, but most, if not all, of the committee, I suspect, realised that I was going to take the option of living elsewhere. In the nine years I was minister of the Abbey, only five people, four of them Abbey members, expressed regret at our decision not to live in the Place of Paisley. The fifth was Mrs Rogan, who never missed a public opportunity to complain that I had abandoned her husband's most important contribution to the life of the Abbey. Fortunately I learned that Bill Rogan's important contributions to the life of Paisley Abbey were not restricted to architectural restoration. Although he regarded himself as a cut above the rest because he was minister of the ancient Abbey, families, from the town's poorest schemes to its middle class villas, spoke with real warmth and affection of Bill Rogan's exemplary pastoral ministry, and although our decision not to live in the Place of Paisley was, I know, a considerable disappointment to him, he was never anything but courteous and friendly towards me, and always grateful for the invitations I extended to him to return to the Abbey and preach.

So, a manse had to be found, and we were left virtually on our own to find somewhere. Fortunately we were able to stay on in the manse of Bellahouston Steven, just seven miles or so from Paisley, while we looked. Once we found somewhere suitable – as it happens the manse of a congregation in the town which had been involved in a union – we were again left virtually on our own to supervise the alterations to it which were required. The use of the minister's residence in the Place of Paisley had meant that the kirk session had in place none of the normal systems to provide and care for a manse. The renovations were in the hands of an old Paisley building firm, and commissioned by an old firm of Paisley lawyers, and complaints about delays or poor workmanship by an incoming minister were not going to interfere with these old Paisley commercial relationships.

My ministry in Paisley Abbey could hardly have had a more

inauspicious start. As was the custom I was "preached in" on my first Sunday by my father, and on the first Sunday evening conducted my first service. Evening services were very poorly attended, and were held in the St Mirin Chapel, which held around sixty. On that first Sunday evening, there were quite a number of empty pews in the chapel. The church officer was excused attendance on Sunday evenings, and as I was preparing to go into the church the elder on duty told me that all the lights had fused. It was a June evening, and just sufficient light was coming through the windows for the congregation to read the words of the hymns. However it was only when I stood up to announce the first of them that I realised how inappropriate it was: "Art thou afraid his power shall fail?"

The following Sunday evening a visiting choir from the United States was leading the worship and so the whole church was used. Torrential rain was pouring down as the service started, and half way through, guttering all round the nave gave way and rain water cascaded into the building. By the time the service was finished, a vast area of the church was under water. A team of "moppers-up" made little impact on the flooded nave and crossing area. When eventually we joined the American choir for coffee after the service, one of the congregation, who had been present on both Sunday evenings, said to me "You'll be wondering what you've come to?"

She was right.

What I had come to, I soon discovered, was a church which faced enormous problems, not the least of which, as was brought forcibly home to me on my first Sundays, was the state of the building. Not only were its gutters in urgent need of replacement, but the stonework of the nave was seriously deteriorating. Generations of industrial pollution, combined with the well above average rainfall of Paisley had produced sulphuric acid which had eaten its way through a good deal of the stone and a large amount of the pointing. Two of the leading lights of the Society of Friends of Paisley Abbey, Jimmie Shaw and Clark Hunter, met with me, almost as soon as I was inducted, to point out that a minimum of half a million pounds was going to be required to preserve the Abbey's future.

A joint committee of the kirk session and the Society of Friends was set up, and very quickly it was decided that there had to be an appeal to raise a sum as large, then, as £500,000. More controversial was the decision to employ a firm of fund-raisers, Craigmyle and Company. There were many who were suspicious of fund-raisers, and who believed that they would take more in fees than they raised in income. There were others who felt that fund-raising should be a matter of running the sort of social events, large-scale concerts, charity dinners, celebrity dances, which would become an essential part of the social calendar for a certain type of Paisley family. However the Society of Friends agreed to underwrite the cost of contracting Craigmyle for a year, and while Craigmyle charged a straight fee (not a percentage of the money raised) they said that their track record showed that their fee would turn out to be around 5% of the money raised.

I suspect that those who supported bringing in a firm of fund-raisers did so for a reason which proved, fortunately, to be totally false. Everyone with whom I discussed the Abbey's deteriorating fabric agreed that the Abbey congregation could not be expected to provide much money itself. Though there were some extremely well-off families in the congregation, the vast majority of the membership was made up of ordinary people who did not have large quantities of surplus money. My guess is that those who wanted to employ fund-raisers assumed that they would raise money for the Abbey without troubling the congregation.

If they did, they were very quickly corrected. From the start, the Appeals Director whom Craigmyle put in post, Iain Mulholland, made two things absolutely clear: there had to be an approach to every member of the congregation, because unless the congregation was shown to have supported the appeal, none of the public bodies, companies and trusts to whom approaches would be later made would pay the slightest attention to our polite requests for help; and secondly there would be no coffee mornings, evening socials, whist drives, dances or any other fund rasing events until all the congregation and local businesses had been contacted, otherwise what Iain Mulholland called the "inoculation factor" would come into play – people who might be expected to make a substantial donation would think that by buying five books of raffle tickets at £1 each, they had sufficiently contributed to the appeal.

A series of around twenty five meetings was arranged in the various areas of Paisley and beyond where the congregation lived: two, sometimes three, each evening. Iain Mulholland said that it was essential to the strategy that, as minister, I had to be present at every meeting. It was certainly a very quick way of meeting the congregation, but not one which I would have chosen! The meetings were held in the homes of members of the congregation, the first of them in late May 1979, just a year after I had been inducted. They were all completed by the time I went on holiday at the end of June, and something in the region of £125,000 had by then been donated or pledged by the congregation, without any drop in the givings for normal congregational purposes. I had always insisted that the restoration appeal was not an alternative to the Sunday offering but in addition to it.

I was, I have to admit, taken completely by surprise. However what I had not understood was the strategic significance of the local meeting, with perhaps twenty people present, listening first to me and then to Iain Mulholland. We were in a decided minority, but if we made our case and succeeded in getting support from just a few at the meeting, others would follow. The other thing I had not grasped was that if we were to be successful in raising the large sum we wanted from the congregation, it could only be done through what were then called deeds of covenant, now Gift Aid, whereby the income tax paid on a charitable donation was repaid to the charity, thereby increasing the value of a donation by, at that time, around 30%.

Two years after the appeal ended, the kirk session decided to use exactly the same means to improve the congregation's ordinary givings. This strategy, based on local meetings and stressing predominantly giving by deeds of covenant was at odds with the strategy adopted by the Church of Scotland in its attempts to increase congregational giving. The Church based its campaigns on visits to members' homes by a team of trained visitors. This approach was, and still is, I believe, flawed on two counts. People who open the door and find visitors from the church wanting to talk to them about money are, I am convinced, immediately put on the defensive, and so are less likely to respond willingly. And even the best-trained visitor is doing something he or she would rather not be doing. Some are downright reluctant. All tend not to push the need for money too seriously. Indeed money is only part of what the Church's official Stewardship strategy stresses: time, talents and money are what the Church says it wants, and then is surprised when lots of people rush to offer time and talents and the money comes a poor third.

Of course, those who are thirled to the Kirk's attitude to stewardship will say that what I was involved in was the raising of money for a building, and a much-loved building at that; and it is always easier to raise money for a building than for the wider and less tangible work of the Church. However, as a result of my experience with Craigmyle, friends in other parishes heard me talk about the strategy adopted, and I found myself being invited to run meetings for office-bearers in churches as far apart as Dumbarton (ironically, Riverside, where my friend Jim Miller was minister) Stirling, Lanark, Aberdeen, and Dundee. In all these congregations campaigns, run on the lines to which Craigmyle had introduced me, produced results above the average for stewardship campaigns. I know that before his early and untimely death, Iain Mulholland had tried to persuade the Church of Scotland Board of Stewardship that his ideas would bear fruit, but he got nowhere with them. I was not surprised.

As the winter of 1979-80 set in, we were engaged in approaching business, trusts, companies with a Paisley connection, and individuals whose support we might expect, but on the basis that the congregation had already raised well over £100,000. On January 31st 1980, we held a public launch of the appeal, by which time £325,000 had been raised, and we were asking the public to contribute to the final stages of what was, by then, clearly going to be a successful appeal. That had, in fact, been the principal strategy: to approach first the congregation, then charitable and commercial institutions, and to appeal to the public directly only when the public would realise that their contributions would be made to an appeal which was going to succeed. By June 1980 I was able to report in a newsletter we sent out to every contributor "We had not expected to pass the £400,000 mark until well into the summer but the total reached to date is £415,000".

Work had already begun on the outside stonework of the west wall, and during the winter of 1980-81 it was planned to replace a false plaster ceiling which had been put up in the nave in the late eighteenth century. Great lumps of the plaster were already falling down. When a previous appeal was launched in 1913 the plaster ceiling was described as having "little artistic merit". Some ribs had been painted on the plaster to give the impression of vaulting, but it was dirty and, a survey indicated, at many points beginning to separate from the wiring and lathes above.

Although the replacement of the ceiling had been included

in all our appeal literature, which had been seen and blessed by the Historic Buildings Council, when we approached the Council for its support – on which support from Renfrew District Council depended – an official of the Council accused us of "vandalism" by destroying a "priceless seventeenth century vaulted plaster ceiling". We pointed out that according to Cameron Lees' magisterial book on Paisley Abbey, at the close of the eighteenth century "the roof was full of holes, through which the birds obtained free access." The "priceless seventeenth century vaulted ceiling" which, we stressed, was a false plaster ceiling, with no vaulting, was erected "as a temporary measure" in the 1780s to address the damage which Cameron Lees described. Please could we have a grant to replace a falling down ceiling "of no artistic merit" with an appropriate, open, wooden roof? The consultant replied by accusing us of destroying "a priceless eighteenth century false plaster ceiling"! The Historic Buildings Council refused to support the work. However, it's an ill wind … Since the Historic Buildings Council refused to regard the new roof as the restoration of an ancient building, we applied to the tax man to declare that it must be "new work". He agreed, and declared it zero rated for VAT which sliced £17,000 off the bill!

Throughout the period when the new roof was being installed, we held services in the choir. In April 1981 we were able to hold a service of thanksgiving, marking the completion of an important phase of the restoration of the Abbey, at which the preacher was the moderator of the General Assembly, Dr Bill Johnston.

Most congregations of the Church of Scotland are run by a kirk session, which deals with the spiritual affairs of the congregation, and a Congregational Board (or in a few remaining cases a Deacons' Court or committee of Management) which handles the temporal business of the congregation. To most people it seems an eminently sensible arrangement, but it is one

I have never been happy with. If nothing divides the sacred from the secular, communion from community, then it is a completely artificial division to separate the spiritual and temporal affairs of a congregation. Decisions about a congregation's spiritual welfare and priorities must be earthed in the practical decisions it takes; and the practical decisions arrived at have spiritual consequences. So I was pleased that the affairs of Paisley Abbey, spiritual and temporal, were in the hands of the kirk session.

When I arrived, the kirk session numbered around seventy of whom one was a woman, Jessie Scott. The session clerk, Alex Leishman, had been an elder since the 1930s, and session clerk since the 1940s, and there was very little I might suggest, or anyone else might propose, but he had seen it suggested and proposed before, and knew it did not work. Although the kirk session gave its complete support to the restoration appeal, Alex Leishman refused to take any part in it.

When the first opportunity to appoint new elders arose, I raised with the kirk session the question of gender. It seemed quite absurd that there should be only one woman on the kirk session and so I explained that when names were being suggested, no account should be taken of gender whatsoever. When the time came for the ordination of new elders, there were several women among them. At a meeting with the new elders just before their ordination, Alex Leishman said that there were several kirk session committees, and perhaps, now that there were so many women on the Session, they should form a tea committee! One of the new elders, who was to become not only the greatest of supporters but the firmest of friends, Jean Craig, fixed him with the sort of fiercely affectionate glare that had frozen recalcitrant children in Paisley Grammar and Ralston Primary: "Alex Leishman, *that* is enough!"

We were never sure when the session clerk was being serious, or mischievous. He was a bachelor school teacher, long retired, who resented any meeting finishing much earlier than 10.00 pm, since he had come out, as he put it "for the night". So he adopted the practice, whenever he felt a meeting was likely to end indecently early (in his view), of raising the most contentious matter, discussion of which would be likely to occupy the meeting well after 10.00 pm. In an attempt to counteract this, I began the practice of insisting that all business for the kirk session should be intimated in advance and placed on the agenda beforehand.

The session clerk's other way of ensuring that Session meetings took quite a time was by writing minutes of inordinate length. My very first kirk session meeting lasted just over half an hour, fully twenty five minutes of which was taken up with the reading of the minutes of the previous meeting. I soon discovered that it usually took nearly half an hour to read the minutes, by which time the glazed looks on the faces of the kirk session indicated that the business of the meeting had lost the attention of the membership, and it would not be regained until some matter of controversy arose. This, I quickly discovered, usually involved either the organist, the organ or the choir.

Paisley Abbey had a long and distinguished tradition of church music, and a tradition, almost as long, of the music causing trouble. After I was elected minister but before I was inducted, the interim moderator phoned and asked to see me urgently. He told me that as a result of a disagreement between the organist and some members of the kirk session and its Psalmody committee, the organist, George McPhee, had tendered his resignation with effect from the end of June. I was due to be inducted at the end of May. What, the interim moderator asked, did I think should be done? I had no wish to lose the services of such a fine organist as George McPhee, but neither did I want the record to show that a month after I had been inducted he had resigned. The implication would be clear, but false. So I said to the interim moderator that he should inform the organist that his resignation was accepted, but would, in fact take effect the day before I was inducted. In the event, the resignation was withdrawn.

I was aware of the tension there was between the organist and some members of the kirk session, and equally aware that the tension focused on the activities of the Psalmody committee, which, as well as dealing with all matters to do with the organist and his contract, and the upkeep of the organ, was responsible for the choir, made up of both adults and boys. Eight of the adults were paid a token sum which, some members of the Psalmody committee appeared to believe, entitled the kirk session to demand their attendance at every service held. "They are being paid" was the constant comment made.

As soon as I was inducted I said to George McPhee that if he agreed not to attend meetings of the Psalmody committee, I would guarantee that he always got a fair deal. I then decided that if the kirk session had to have a Psalmody committee, then I would have to make it clear at the first meeting I attended, that the whole of worship, including the music, was the sole preserve of the minister, and that whatever members of the committee might think, or want to do, they would have to deal with me and not with the organist. I also determined that at the earliest possible moment I would ensure that I took over the chair of the Psalmody committee.

The root of the problem was something which permeated almost all of Paisley Abbey's life. It had an organist and choir of national and international reputation, but there were those who made sure they knew to whom they were answerable. In the same way I discovered that there were some in Paisley Abbey who liked to think of themselves as one of the most important congregations in the land, but who wanted to run the congregation on a shoe-string. There was a secretary two hours a day, whose main jobs were to send out the account for weddings and send in the weekly notice to the *The Glasgow Herald*. There seemed genuine amazement when I suggested that the administration of a congregation and building the size of Paisley Abbey required rather more than that. I was shocked to discover that the monthly congregational magazine was duplicated on an ancient machine kept in the session clerk's house. There was an amateurism about the way the congregation was run, which contrasted with the professional reputation which the organist had, quite rightly, and which was perhaps resented. So there was the constant tension, which led one member of the Psalmody committee to tell me, shortly after I went to the Abbey as minister, that he could handle an application for a loan amounting to a million eurodollars before coffee, but Paisley Abbey's Psalmody committee had him on valium!

I believed, wrongly as I now realise, that if there was an area of trouble and tension in the life of the congregation it was my job to take entire responsibility, as far as I could, for the part of the congregation's life which was causing the trouble, and to make sure it caused trouble no longer. And the reason I took that view was, of course, that I believed that if there was tension within a congregation it was my fault for not preventing it.

Quite apart from failing to realise that music had been a source of conflict in Paisley Abbey since long before I was born, I also did not recognise that however laudable my aim was, it was going to suck me inexorably into petty conflicts and personality squabbles in which I would be assumed to have taken one side or another. I needed to learn that I had been called to be the minister, not the suffering servant, bearing on my shoulders all their iniquities! But until that realisation dawned on me, I went home after each meeting, unable to sleep over the conflicts which I had not been able to prevent. Meanwhile I smiled bravely and pretended I was able to handle it all!

For me, and my ministry in Paisley Abbey, matters came to a head over the church officer. The church officer when I was inducted had held the post for nearly twenty years, and was hugely popular with those who spent a lot of time in and around the Abbey buildings. He was not, however, as fit as he once had been and even with the assistance which had been provided for him, he was finding the duties too much, and decided to retire. We advertised for a successor, and appointed someone much younger, who was provided with living accommodation for himself, his wife and son in a wing of the former minister's residence in the Place of Paisley. He started work with great energy and enthusiasm, and people began to notice quite a change. Woodwork began to shine, brasses began to sparkle, floors were clean. We all thought that we had made a good choice. He coped admirably in the difficult circumstances during the winter of 1980-81 when the roof of the ceiling of the nave was replaced, and, inevitably, despite heavy sheeting to block off the nave area, dust and dirt was a permanent problem.

In September 1981, the church officer took ill with what initially appeared to be flu. He was then admitted to the neurosurgical unit of the Southern General Hospital and, I was told by his wife, diagnosed as suffering from *myasthenia gravis*, a progressively deteriorating muscular disease. The day after he was released from hospital, he explained that the problem from which he suffered meant that in the mornings he was lethargic, but by the evenings he felt fully fit. I suggested to him that the kirk session might agree to a flexi-hours arrangement. Later he said to me that, rather than accepting the offer of a flexi-hours arrangement, he would prefer to come back to work for the normal hours, but be restricted to "light duties". I consulted with the kirk session's Property Convener, and then told the church officer that our view was that he should not return to work until he was capable of undertaking all the duties of church officer, light and heavy. We had in the meantime been advised by a doctor who was a member of the kirk session, that if someone suffering from *myasthenia gravis* undertook heavy duties he could do severe damage to himself. The kirk session's Property committee agreed that there was a danger that if allowed back to work for "light duties" the church officer might do more than he should, and we, as his employers, would be liable. I did not want to take the risk of frightening the church officer with the prospect of doing himself serious damage, and so expressed the Property committee's view simply as requiring him to be fit for all duties before he returned to work. The following day he submitted a doctor's certificate saying that he was unfit for work because he was suffering from *myasthenia gravis*, and he was off work until February, when he returned to his full duties.

Had I known what was to transpire I would not have dealt personally with the church officer. But at the time I had no reason to assume that I was dealing with anything more contentious than the pastoral care of a member of the congregation who happened also to be an employee of the kirk session. However, by the time he returned to work full-time, the church officer had clearly become convinced that I was personally responsible for conducting some kind of vendetta against him. I was so concerned about this that, on the advice of the kirk session, I told him that because of his attitude I could not risk matters being further personalised and that the kirk session's dealings with him would be through its Property Convener. Meanwhile I was advised to keep my own dealings with him to a minimum, and always to keep a written record of them. However these steps, which were intended to distance the minister personally from decisions taken about the church officer, merely further fuelled his antagonism towards me.

Shortly after the church officer returned to work, the Abbey was officially informed by the Paisley Job Centre that the church officer was registered as disabled and he was capable only of performing "light duties". The kirk session suspended the church officer for two weeks on full pay, and with his permission wrote to his doctor, a member of the congregation, Dr Robert Bannatyne, who confirmed that he suffered from *myasthenia gravis*, and that he was unfit to undertake any tasks which involved prolonged muscular effort. At its next meeting the kirk session took the view that the church officer was unfit to perform his duties and with regret felt that it could no longer employ him, and gave him eight weeks to leave the house in the Place of Paisley.

Almost immediately the church officer indicated that he proposed to appeal to an industrial tribunal. The kirk session instructed a legal firm with expertise in industrial law to act on its behalf. What neither I nor the kirk session knew, however, was that before Dr Bannatyne's confirmation that the church officer suffered from *myasthenia gravis* and was unfit for duties which involved sustained muscular effort, the medical practice where he was a partner had received a letter from a consultant in the Southern General Hospital, indicating that the church officer was not, in fact, suffering from the disease.

While giving evidence for over three hours on the first day of the industrial tribunal I was shown this letter and it was put to me that the kirk session had known all along that the diagnosis of *myasthenia gravis* was false, that it had dismissed the church officer out of spite and that he should be re-instated. When I said, truthfully, that neither I nor any member of the kirk session was aware of the letter, I was asked if I really expected the tribunal to believe that a doctor would confirm a diagnosis which his practice had been formally notified by a consultant was wrong.

When the tribunal suspended for the day, our solicitor told myself, and the kirk session's representative, Wallace Neil, that the only hope of salvaging anything from both the case and our reputations was to persuade Dr Bannatyne that he had made a serious error in his letter to the kirk session and to give evidence to that effect. However, our solicitor said that Dr Bannatyne was under no obligation to do so, and that if he was giving the doctor advice, he would recommend that he admit nothing and refuse to give evidence. However our solicitor had not reckoned with Dr Bannatyne's integrity.

The three of us, Wallace Neil, our solicitor and myself drove to Dr Bannatyne's home where we explained to him that his letter confirming the church officer's diagnosis had been written after a consultant's letter had been sent to his practice giving a contrary opinion. Dr Bannatyne said he would make investigations at his surgery and contact us later. Later that evening he confirmed that it was one of his partners who had referred the church officer to the Southern General and had received the results. Dr Bannatyne had not seen the letter and so he continued to confirm a diagnosis which had been rejected by the consultant. He would willingly come to the tribunal and explain that he had misled the kirk session.

When the tribunal closed, our solicitor's advice was that Dr Bannatyne's evidence had cleared both myself and the kirk session of the most serious charge against us but that in all likelihood we would lose the case because, technically, we should have had one further meeting with the church officer confronting him again with the diagnosis, and he would then have been bound to show us the consultant's letter. However, his legal view was that there would be very little compensation payable and we would not be asked to reinstate the church officer. He warned us that we would receive a one-line indication of the tribunal's verdict which might well give rise to wild speculation. As it did. "Abbey beadle wins his case" ran one headline. "Victory for man sacked at Abbey" ran another. While the church officer claimed that he would receive thousands of pounds in compensation, I tried to discourage any reaction until we received the tribunal's determination in full. When we did, the kirk session was criticised, as we knew it would be, for failing to hold a meeting with the church officer to confirm the diagnosis, but any question of reinstatement was ruled out. The church officer was criticised for "insulting" and "unacceptable" behaviour. And compensation was set at just over £260.

The whole business lasted just under a year, and for the first, but not the last time in my life I found myself being treated for depression. Early on I realised how serious for the church, and how bad for myself, it would be if I continued to take the lead in discussions and decisions, but even by then the sort of dominant leadership style I had developed had come to be expected in the Abbey. On several occasions I asked the kirk session to find ways of ensuring that I was distanced from the issues which were increasingly publicised. I always received support but never sensed that anyone understood that what I was trying to say was that I needed to be protected not just from the church officer but from myself! I needed space and distance to develop a different, and much healthier, approach to the ministry. I had to start allowing the human being behind the mask to be the minister of Paisley Abbey, instead of projecting an image which was designed to shield the human being all the time.

Looking back I can identify important stages on the way to developing not just a different attitude to ministry but a transformed view of Christian faith.

Twice, once in the middle of the controversy and then when it was over, I explained to the kirk session that I simply could not go on. I was emotionally exhausted and needed time for rest. So I was taking sick leave. I would never before have admitted, within the church, that I was unable to cope, and I hope admitting it was done in a straightforward way without any sense of self-indulgence. It was just a matter of fact, but it was the sort of fact I had refused to face before.

As soon as the Industrial Tribunal had issued the reasons for its decision, I telephoned the elder on the kirk session who had been most critical of the decisions made and of myself personally, and asked him to have lunch with me so that a relationship which had been fairly cordial before the church officer's case arose could be restored. It may seem strange that it took me until this stage in my ministry to realise that it was part of my calling to take the initiative to ensure that relationships were not allowed to be soured by disagreements. I always knew the theory; for the first time I realised I could not live with myself if I did not put it into practice, even if rebuffed, which in this case it was not.

In the course of the year of controversy, I tried, from the pulpit, to draw lessons which only very occasionally, and quite unjustifiably, became a defence of what the kirk session had done. (Preaching during this period was not made easy by the church officer sitting right under the pulpit glaring throughout every service) More typically, I hope, I tried to point out that the letters of Paul were written to address difficulties, tensions, conflicts within the churches to which he wrote, and that in Paisley Abbey we should be trying to "do theology together" as we reflected on and worked our way through a serious problem.

Most importantly, however, I began to reflect for the first time on the importance of "vulnerability" as an important theme in the Christian Gospel: the vulnerability of all Christian action to misinterpretation and misunderstanding and the vulnerability of every response of Christian love which inherently includes the possibility of its own rejection.

So, as I approached five years as minister of Paisley Abbey, I decided the time was right to try to explain that I thought my attitude to the ministry had changed. On the fifth anniversary of my induction I reflected on what I had learned.

"In the past five years" I said, "you have taught me that it is far more important to struggle, not to harbour bitterness and resentment, to try to resist the temptation not to forgive, than it is to have a doctrinally precise understanding of forgiveness.

In the past five years you have taught me that it is far more important, when you are faced with despair and depression, to hold on to the belief that God never abandons us, that Good

Friday and Easter Day for a Christian are not past events but present experience, than it is to imagine that you have got the Resurrection neatly summed up.

You have taught me in the past five years that faith is something which keeps you alive, and that's much more important than it is to be able to sign your name on a dotted line at the foot of the Apostles' Creed or the Westminster Confession of Faith, or any of the other formulae beloved of the Church.

You have taught me that it is more important to believe that God was in Christ spelling out that we are all one because Christ became one with us, than it is to be able to answer exactly the question whether Jesus was human or divine or both.

You have taught me to look again at the New Testament, and, whatever the scholars may say about it, to recognise in the New Testament words written by people wrestling with precisely the same problems as we have had to wrestle with, and having to take decisions remarkably similar to the decisions that we have had to take from time to time. And I see in the New Testament a reflection of the wrestling and the discussion rather than a set of definitive answers to everything.

You have taught me that the Church is people on a journey of discovery, exploring what difference it makes to their lives to call God Father, and who believe that in Jesus we see what God is like. The Church is people discovering what difference it makes to their lives to believe that forgiveness is a better way than resentment, that despair somehow is never able to obliterate hope, that faith is often one side of a coin whose other side is doubt, that despite differences and disagreements Christians are all one in the One who beckons them on this journey saying 'Follow me' ".

During these first five years in the Abbey, one of the elders had gone from being initially very welcoming of the new minister to disliking me intensely. He told me once that he had decided that he would oppose absolutely everything I proposed. On Sunday mornings he took to remaining seated, while the congregation remained standing, as I processed out of the church with the choir. It is not exaggerating, I think, to say that he hated me. To this day I do not know why. I must admit I was very relieved when I heard that he and his wife were moving away from Paisley, even although I was told that he would continue his membership of the Abbey. He and his wife turned up from time to time but his glare on these rare visits was not too difficult to put up with.

Then, one day during a Holy Week, I was told that his wife had been diagnosed as suffering from terminal cancer, and did not have long to live. She was extremely unlikely to survive until the summer, when one of her children was to be married in the Abbey by another minister, a family friend.

I do not think of myself as a particularly pious person, nor as someone who is intensely aware of God speaking, but throughout the rest of the Holy Week I knew that if I believed at all what I had been saying each evening, I had to make the journey to see this elder and his wife.

At the beginning of the following week I set off, feeling less than comfortable. I think I began to drive more slowly as I approached the town. I found the house and rang the bell. When the door was answered I was confronted by a man who was clearly surprised to see me.

"What do you want?" he asked.

I said that I had heard about his wife, that whatever had happened in the past I was still his minister and I had come to see if there was anything at all that I could do.

"I suppose you'd better come in."

He took me into his living room and asked me to sit down while he went to see whether his wife wanted to see me. A short while later he came back and said that she did, and he left me with her.

She and I talked for I suppose twenty minutes and then she said, "Would you do something for me? Would you give me communion?"

I had neither bible nor service book with me, but her husband brought some sherry in a glass and a piece of bread, and somehow I got through a version of the communion service. It probably would not have passed strict theological examination, but it was no time for strict theology. Later on, I asked if he would mind if I came back again, and he said that he thought his wife would appreciate it.

The next time I went, the patient seemed a bit better. Each time I visited, she seemed less weak. She was told that the cancer had stopped growing so quickly. And each time I visited, her husband seemed less hostile. The couple moved back much nearer Paisley and although she was left in no doubt that her illness was terminal, she was no longer bed ridden. She even danced at the wedding.

I was with her two days before she died in hospital almost exactly a year from my first visit. Her death occurred when I was on holiday for a week and the funeral was arranged for the day after my return.

I tell that story not because of any pride in what I did, and certainly not because I imagine that giving someone communion was a turning point in her disease. I tell it because if, at any time in my ministry before then, something similar had happened, I would not have made the journey to that bedside. I would have believed that the estrangement had been nothing to do with me, and that it had been made clear to me that my ministry was not welcomed.

But Paisley Abbey, and the tension and pain there, had taught me that the only way I could survive was by trying to live out in the way I worked what I said when I preached: that a vulnerable God invites us to share our vulnerability with him, and so in dying we live.

6

Within a week or so of becoming minister of Paisley Abbey, there was a performance of Bach's *B Minor Mass*. It was the first time I had heard the work, and I can recall very vividly the feeling of being totally overwhelmed, as the choir and orchestra burst into the *Sanctus*. If I were ever asked to contribute to a programme which used to be on Radio 4, *The Tingle Factor*, (like all brilliant ideas for radio programmes so obvious once you've heard it!), the "Sanctus" from Bach's *B Minor Mass* would be at the top of the list of pieces of music which make the hairs on the back of my neck stand up and the tingle factor get to work.

When I arrived at the Abbey that Saturday night, I was told that I would be expected either at the beginning or towards the end of the performance to invite the audience to join in prayer. That, I was told, was what would turn a concert into an act of worship. I refused, for two reasons, one of them important, the other trivial. The important reason was that it seemed to me that no prayer by me was likely to lead the audience into the presence of God more effectively than the music of J.S. Bach. And when I had heard the work I was more convinced of that than I was at the start. The trivial reason was that it reminded me too much of something which used to happen regularly in my father's church of Stevenson Memorial in Glasgow, where, when I was a young boy in the choir, there used to be annual performances of Handel's *Messiah*. My father was virtually tone deaf and had little interest in music. However he was expected to sit in the pulpit throughout the performance, which he did, surreptitiously reading a book throughout, until I gave him the pre-arranged signal immediately before the last chorus of *Messiah*. I coughed loudly three times, and this was the cue for him to stand up and offer a prayer before the performance concluded. It seemed a ludicrous intrusion into a musical performance and I did not want to repeat it.

I was privileged to enjoy some wonderful musical experiences in the Abbey, none more so than a performance of Bach's *St John Passion,* in which Sir Peter Pears sang the part of the Evangelist, and there was a star studded cast of soloists including Neil Mackie, Peter Morrison and Linda Finnie. The performance was in aid of the Abbey's Restoration Appeal and was sponsored by the (then) Trustee Savings Bank. It was not just an unforgettable occasion in an Abbey packed to capacity, it was a learning experience for me in coaxing money from a company like the Trustee Savings Bank. I was told by one of its top managers that the Bank did not make straight donations to causes such as the Abbey's Appeal. It would, however, sponsor events such as a concert. I explained that our experience in the Abbey tended to be that concerts seldom made the amount of money expected because the costs rose as the concert drew near. Patiently I was told that what the Bank had in mind was this: I would approach some of the top singers and ask them how much they would normally charge to sing a particular role. I would then persuade them to come and sing for a considerably smaller sum, but the Bank would contribute to the Appeal fund the amount which the artist would have charged. So I set about my task. With a considerable amount of help from the tenor Neil Mackie, who had been brought up in the Abbey choir, we persuaded Sir Peter Pears, whose fee would usually have been in excess of £2000, to sing for £500. So already the Appeal fund was at least £1500 better off. I recall telephoning the Scots singers Peter Morrison and Helen McArthur, both of whom I had known at university, and persuading them to sing for virtually nothing. When I spoke to Peter I said "I know you could usually charge £500 but would you agree to sing for £100" "Johnston" Peter said, "for the privilege of singing with Pears I would pay you £100!" I did not take him up on it!

Paisley Abbey's choir introduced me to so much music which has now become part of my life. In 1982 we were making a series of television programmes for BBC Scotland, in one of which I was joined by a group of the kirk session, as I talked to them and the camera about what the role of the Abbey might be. The recordings took place in the week after Easter. I had been involved in services all through Holy Week and on Easter Day, and had then gone off to spend two nights leading an Edinburgh church youth group's conference in the borders. I got back on the Tuesday evening for the first recording very, very tired and, for the first time heard another version of the *Sanctus*, from Fauré's *Requiem*. The next day I went out and bought a record of the whole *Requiem*. But the *Sanctus* remains my favourite section of it.

I will always associate two very amusing moments with the series of television programmes we made in the spring of 1982. In one of the programmes, the producer/director Les Mitchell decided that he would take his cameras into a pub in Paisley and get reactions to the Abbey. One punter on being asked what he thought of Paisley Abbey replied that he thought it was a museum, and another, asked whether he would ever consider becoming a member of the Abbey congregation said "You can't just join Paisley Abbey: there's a waiting list"!

One of the programmes made was for *Songs of Praise*. I had lunch with the producer, from London, and a researcher, and talked about the kind of people who might be interviewed in the programme. One of the Abbey's elders, a middle manager in the textile industry, had been made redundant the previous year. He ran the home, and his wife returned to teaching, and the two of them had managed to cope with the trauma of redundancy. I was not so naïve as to assume that this was a universal recipe for surviving unemployment but I thought it might be a helpful signal to send, that there were sometimes creative ways of responding. The researcher went off and spent an afternoon with the couple. The next time we met I asked her how she had got on. "They are terrific" she said "but we couldn't possibly use them in the programme" "Why on earth not?" I asked. "Because they are too happy"! I thought that was a very revealing comment about what was then looked for in *Songs of Praise*. Today things are very different. The more exotic, trendy and down-market the setting the more it appeals to today's *Songs of Praise* producers.

The Abbey had its fair share of special services, two of which I will never forget. One was a service to mark the fortieth anniversary of the YMCA. The preacher at the service was to be the moderator of the General Assembly that year, Professor John McIntyre, who some months earlier had welcomed the Pope on the steps of the General Assembly Hall. (In passing I might mention that, quite recently, my friend and broadcasting colleague Colin Mackay told me that he had been commentating on the event for STV, who had microphones strategically placed, near the group of Assembly worthies gathered on the top of the steps to greet the Pope. According to Colin, the microphones picked up one of the group, Dr Peter Brodie, on being introduced saying to John Paul II saying "You'll remember me, your Holiness, we met at your induction"!)

Also among the clergy taking part in the YMCA's anniversary service was the then Bishop of Paisley, Stephen MacGill. We processed into the Cathedral behind the choir. Just as we took our places, and the organ voluntary drew to a quiet close, Pastor Jack Glass and at least one of his supporters rose from the congregation and began shouting. I could not make out what was being said because as soon as he realised what was happening, George McPhee smartly pulled out all the stops, drowning out the shouts as the protesters were led out by some of the kirk session. I moved across the chancel to where Bishop MacGill was sitting and apologised to him for the discourtesy of what I had taken to be a protest at the presence of a Roman Catholic bishop. He simply smiled and said "Oh they're not protesting about me: they're protesting about the moderator having met the Pope". So I turned then to John McIntyre and apologised to him. "Oh, it's nothing to do with me" he said, "they're having a go at the Roman Catholic bishop!"

The moderator of a few years later figures in the other special service I will not forget. It was held to mark the centenary of Dr Barnardo's homes, and the moderator that year was Dr Robert Craig. Robert Craig's career as a university teacher and administrator in southern Africa had done nothing to diminish his Fife accent, and the forty or fifty cigarettes he smoked each day had given his voice a deep gravelly tone. He was to preach, followed by a civic reception in Paisley Town Hall, just across the road from the Abbey. The service itself passed uneventfully, as did the civic reception. At the end of it I went home to prepare a sermon for another special service the next day – to mark the fiftieth anniversary of the Scottish Women's Bowling Association! I was sitting at my desk when the telephone rang.

"Johnston, it's Bob Craig"

"Yes, moderator. What can I do for you?"

"I'm being driven home. I'm at Harthill, and I've just discovered I don't have the ring. I've lost the ring!" he said despairingly.

Each moderator of the General Assembly hands over to his successor a large gold ring with a huge purple stone set in it. This ring had been the gift to his successors by the moderator of the General Assembly in 1907, Dr James Mitford Mitchell, who, thirty years earlier had been a minister in Paisley Abbey. This was the ring which the moderator told me he had lost. He went on to say that, on the following day, he was due to go to Iona with other church leaders and it would be a "terrible shame" if the ring was lost. "Would you go down to the Town Hall and see if you can find it?"

I set off down to the Town Hall and made myself extremely unpopular with the local authority staff, by asking them to recall all the table cloths and napkins from the laundry and to go through them in search of the ring. I made myself even more unpopular with the kitchen staff, by asking them to go through all the slops and remains in the waste bins to see if, somehow, the ring had been scooped up with the waste. No ring was found. I telephoned the Principal Clerk of the General Assembly, James Weatherhead, and told him what had happened, and he advised me that, since there might have to be an insurance claim, I had better report the loss of the ring to the police. So I made my way to the main Paisley Police Station on the other side of the Abbey from the Town Hall.

I said to the policewoman at the desk "There's this important guy in the Church of Scotland called the moderator, and he wears a muckle big ring. He's just been to a lunch in the Town Hall, and phoned me to say that the ring has been lost, and I thought I'd better report it."

"Would that be the big purple ring that's just been handed in?" the policewoman asked.

"Yes, where was it found?"

"Oh, someone found it in the gutter outside the Town Hall and handed it in."

I was told that, if I handed over £20, I could have the ring back.

After a visit to a cash dispenser, I had the ring in my pocket and went back home to phone the moderator. I told him I had the ring and where it had been found.

"Och!" he said, "I know what's happened. I'm not much of a ring man myself, and so I take the thing off whenever I can and put it in the pocket of my breeches. I was being driven back to Edinburgh in a wee car and as I got into the front seat the ring must have slipped out of my pocket".

I said to the moderator that I had to go to a meeting that

evening, but it would be finished by about nine o'clock and I would drive straight through to Edinburgh so that he would have the ring for his visit to Iona the next day.

"When will you be here? About ten o'clock. Well I'll be in bed but my wife will stay up for you."

Just after ten o'clock that evening I arrived at the moderator's residence. I handed the ring over to Mrs Craig, who thanked me, and I drove back to Paisley. I still had to find something to say to the Scottish Women's Bowling Association!

When I first met with George McPhee after arriving at the Abbey I suggested to him that we might have a monthly service of choral evensong and invite the two Episcopal congregations to join us. After a year the three of us took it in turns to preach. Even before I went to the Abbey I had been a regular listener to Choral Evensong on Radio 3, and it was a great joy, when minister in Paisley, to take part in many Radio 3 broadcasts of Evensong. My predecessor James Ross had been a great singer (and indeed Precentor of the General Assembly) and in his day when Evensong came from the Abbey he was the precentor. I drew the line, however, at singing, allowing my late father to say caustically that he had discovered the one thing I would not do for the BBC for a fee! Many years later I made a programme with Ian Mackenzie for Radio 4 about Choral Evensong called *Just a Song at Twilight* which won the Runner-up-Award in the prestigious Sandford St Martin Prize in 1994.

Two moments in the production of that programme will remain with me. One was standing on York Station with Ian Mackenzie and suddenly realising that the station announcer was chanting the places to be called at by the next train ... "calling at Doncaster, Newark, Peterborough (change here for March and Cambridge) and London King's Cross"... in exactly the style of a precentor at Choral Evensong ... "O Lord open thou our lips ... and our hearts shall shew forth thy praise." There and then Ian and I decided that the only way to begin our programme was to mix from a real Choral Evensong to the sing-song voice of the announcer at York Station.

The other moment was in the little village of East Acklam in North Yorkshire. I had heard that the distinguished organist of York Minster, Dr Francis Jackson, had retired there, and on a Sunday evening in the local church was playing an old pedal harmonium for choral evensong. I decided that if choral evensong was such a vital part of English culture that a famous organist would accompany a congregation on a harmonium, this had to be recorded. So we made arrangements on a Sunday evening to record in their little parish church. There were twelve people present (including the vicar and Dr Francis Jackson). There was no choir, only a congregation, consisting of eight women and four men, and of the four women one sang bass and the other tenor. The men sang no part recognisable to us. We recorded the entire service, with the intention of using just a snatch or two of the recording to illustrate how deeply ingrained in English country life the experience of choral evensong is. I sat in a tiny van outside the church, happy that we were going to capture something culturally authentic about English life (which John Major was later to compare to "warm beer and a spinster cycling through the mist to early morning communion") when I heard the vicar explain to the congregation how thrilling it was that we were recording their service of choral evensong for transmission at a later date on Radio 3.

I hope he is not still listening out for the broadcast!

However, back in time to Paisley Abbey.

In April 1982, the government led by Mrs Thatcher declared war on Argentina over its occupation of the Falkland Islands.

I am, and have always been a pacifist, but I am well aware that my position is neither the only nor even the majority view held by Christians. However, I have always thought that when Jesus said "forgive your enemies" he was not talking metaphorically, and that when St Paul wrote that "the weakness of God is stronger than men" he was not writing theoretically. So, when we experience violence as a country, the Christian response is to look for ways to forgive and to regard the apparently weak way of non-violence as its appropriate reaction. So, a few weeks after the Falklands campaign began I decided that I had to preach a sermon indicating that my view was that the war could not be justified in Christian terms. However, I stressed on at least three occasions in the sermon that this was my personal view, and that I was speaking personally because I did not want to insist that what I had to say was the only Christian view. Later that evening I agreed to go on BBC Scotland television and attempt to justify my position.

I have always said that if a minister wants to preach controversial sermons, he had better have been regularly in the homes of his congregation. In Paisley Abbey I had continued my Bellahouston practice of systematic congregational visitation, and so, while there were many people who disagreed with what I said about the Falklands War, very few were openly hostile. This I attribute to the fact that most people had got to know me as a person and so saw what I had said through the contacts I had with them. There were a few who took grave exception to what I said, and I understood their criticisms and their standpoint. I took some comfort from the fact that two or three days before I preached the sermon I had told my father, a former army chaplain, what I was going to say. He asked to see the sermon when it was written, and after reading it said to me "You're wrong, and I disagree with you. But you've not given anybody who disagrees with you a reason for thinking you've said they aren't Christian." What he said was some comfort when people said exactly that.

One of my roles as minister of Paisley Abbey was to be chaplain of Paisley Grammar School. The Rector at the time, Bob Corbett, told me that I was expected to turn up every Friday morning and speak to an assembly of the whole school, and so on the first Friday of the autumn term in 1978 I turned up to face the entire school, standing either on the floor of the assembly hall or on one of the three balconies which ringed it. Bob Corbett and I marched into the hall from his study and I announced the hymn I had been told to announce, and the school orchestra launched into the introduction. Once the hymn was finished I spoke for about two minutes, said a prayer of a couple of sentences and Bob Corbett read some school notices and we marched back to his study.

"Fine" he said when I had shut the door behind me. "Fine. But I expect ten minutes from you on a Friday morning."

I said quietly that I thought a two minute talk was more appropriate, and then added "But I'll not tell you how to run the school if you don't tell me how to talk to the Assembly".

From that moment Bob Corbett and I became the firmest of friends. He is dead now, and I was proud to be asked to pay tribute to him at his funeral. But I still miss him like hell.

He was famous for what became known as "Corbettisms". On one occasion, at an assembly I heard him say "As Jesus Christ said, and on this occasion, I think quite rightly, …" At another Assembly we all had to keep our composure when he said, after announcing that a new school scarf had been designed and was available, "So anyone who wants it can get it off Jane Pinkerton in the girl prefects' room"! At a spring performance by the school of "Brigadoon", Bob got up at the interval to express his appreciation, etc. The waves of artificial mist were still hanging over the stage as he emerged above them to speak to the audience. "I hope you can all see a small part of me…" he said, somewhat ambiguously.

One of the pleasures of these weekly assemblies was that two people (who became the closest of friends of mine) worked in the music department at Paisley Grammar School, and conducted the school orchestra: first Irene Doole as a teacher and then her husband Martin as Principal Teacher. They were to see me through the darkest days I would know.

In the autumn of 1982, the minister of Paisley High Kirk, Jack Robertson, telephoned me to say that he was giving up the parish ministry to work in a Family Rehabilitation Unit at Westercraigs in Glasgow, run by the Church of Scotland's Board of Social Responsibility. I had known Jack for ten years or so. He was a fine preacher and a good minister, and he had caused me one of my most embarrassing moments in Paisley presbytery. A few years earlier he told me that a branch of the Gay Switchboard, a telephone counselling service for homosexuals, was opening in Paisley. He had been asked to go along to the opening of the service and wondered whether I would be willing to go with him to give him moral support. I immediately agreed.

This invitation came just a few weeks after the conversation I have already described with a gay man after a broadcast on *Prayer Desk*. I knew I could not refuse, though I think I would have had second thoughts, had I realised that when the day dawned Jack Robertson was not going to turn up at the Gay Switchboard. I was introduced as a Church of Scotland minister and I spoke briefly about being there because I wanted those involved to know that the Christians I spoke for wanted as much support as possible to be given to this venture. Then a photograph was taken of all of us who spoke. This appeared a few days later in the *Paisley Daily Express*, saying, wrongly, that I had been present "representing the presbytery of Paisley".

At the next meeting of the presbytery, an angry elder, waving a copy of that edition of the *Paisley Daily Express*, demanded that I be rebuked and that the presbytery issue a statement saying not only that I was not representing the presbytery at the opening of the Gay Switchboard but that the presbytery regarded homosexuality as .... well, you can imagine what he wanted the presbytery to say about homosexuality. After a short debate I was invited to speak. I told the story of the man who had telephoned me after "Prayer Desk", who had wanted to speak to a voice he only knew through the radio and to whom he felt he could divulge neither his name nor where he lived. I also recalled that after the most recent occasion on which the General Assembly had debated homosexuality, and reached a conclusion which was widely interpreted as critical, the number of those seeking help from the Church of Scotland's counselling centre at Simpson House in Edinburgh had dropped to almost nil. The presbytery declined either to criticise me or to express the asked-for condemnation of homosexuality.

All of that happened a year or so before Jack Robertson told me that he was giving up the parish ministry. He asked me if I would be willing to be interim moderator in the vacancy, and I agreed. He and his wife left the manse and occupied a flat in the Kirk's Westercraigs Family Rehabilitation Centre.

Just a few weeks later I was told that he had had a breakdown, left the flat he and his wife had occupied and was in a psychiatric hospital near Leicester, from where he had written a letter of resignation to the Kirk's Board of Social Responsibility. It so happened that the next week I was due to go to London as chairman, then, of the BBC's Scottish Religious Advisory committee, and I checked that the BBC would cover my expenses if I chose to break my journey near Leicester to visit Jack. He had indeed had a severe breakdown but was beginning to look forward to the possibility that he might return to Scotland. But he had resigned and burned his boats.

As soon as I got home I telephoned the Director of Social Work for the Board of Social Responsibility, explained that Jack had been in no condition to write a serious letter of resignation, and expressed the hope that his letter might be ignored. I can still recall the Director's chilly response. "He has resigned and his resignation has been accepted, but we will always have a pastoral concern for our former employees."

Here was a minister who had resigned when in mental crisis

and his employers, representing the Church he had served as a parish minister for twenty four years, could only say that they had a continuing pastoral concern for a former employee. Jack had no job to return to. Indeed it was doubtful whether he was fit to work. But because he had resigned from the parish ministry after twenty four and not twenty five years he was not entitled to receive his meagre minister's pension until he was seventy. I telephoned Tom Balfour in the Board of Ministry, told him the story, reported the reaction of the Board of Social Responsibility and asked if there was any way Jack could be allowed to take up his pension. Rules were bent, decisions were taken, and within twenty four hours I was able to write to Jack to say that when he felt able to return home he would receive a pension from the Church.

I suppose in every institution there is tension between those at the centre of the organisation, and those in the field, who perceive themselves to be at the periphery. Ever since I became a minister there has been suspicion and criticism of those who work in the central administration of the Church of Scotland. While I was at Paisley Abbey, I was asked by the BBC to present a film about the church's administration based at 121 George Street in Edinburgh. May Bowie, who directed the programme, created an opening sequence in which the camera quickly panned along the front of the building, and then across the roof, creating the impression of a threatening, Kremlin-like structure; that is how it is viewed by many. All through my ministry, the level of criticism has increased, and it seemed to me that a great deal of it came from ministers and congregations who found the perceived failings or insensitivities of those at the centre of the church's administration a convenient scapegoat to blame for the church's decline. In recent years, however, I have sensed a qualitative difference in the relationship between the church's bureaucracy and the congregations.

At the time of writing, around 200 congregations in the

Church of Scotland are providing the funds not only to pay for their own minister but to the funds which make up the shortfalls in congregations which cannot afford to pay their minister in full. A few years ago I began to sense that those "successful" congregations were becoming convinced that only by increasingly devoting their resources to their own survival would their future be guaranteed. They had begun to realise that Church of Scotland plc was not going to be in a position to save them from decline. I suspect I was not alone in making that judgment. I suspect that powerful figures at the centre of the church's committee structure had begun to realise that something of the sort was taking place in the parishes which had traditionally been the biggest givers. So legislation was promoted at the General Assembly which ensured that any failure to contribute the annual assessment would be met with punitive sanctions. If a congregation failed to meet its assessment then, when there was a vacancy, that congregation would not be allowed to call a minister until all the shortfalls had been made up.

It seems to me that, faced with an inevitable financial crisis, those at the centre have reacted in the way all institutions under threat react: by strengthening control from the centre. This is seen in the decision to insist that every presbytery must draw up a plan which will indicate what it expects to happen to every congregation within the presbytery ten years from now: whether a congregation will be allowed a minister of its own, or be linked with another, or be united with one or more congregations. My objection is not to the need for presbyteries to plan, but the insistence that a plan must have the approval of a central committee on Parish Appraisal. I am sure that the defence of the committee will be that if its approval was not required, presbyteries simply would not plan. However what I sense is the conviction that, without centralised control, those in the field cannot be trusted, the typical institutional response to threat.

I have, however, another more fundamental objection to the plan. It assumes that what is important is to decide the fate of congregations on the basis of how they will relate to an ordained minister of word and sacrament. The decision at the end of ten years is to be whether congregations may be given permission to call an ordained minister, or are to be linked with another congregation, and so share an ordained minister, or to be continued as a vacancy, until it can be decided how they will be provided with an ordained minister.

But I see no reason why congregations which cannot themselves support a minister should not be allowed to continue, if they can find people to fill the pulpit and to meet the pastoral needs of the congregation. I would agree that if the time came when, instead of contributing they would require to be supported from central funds, then that would be the time to say to such a congregation that its survival was questionable. But up until that point, what harm does it do to allow the congregation to continue?.

A good friend and colleague of mine, Findlay Turner, the first elder to be moderator of the presbytery of Ardrossan, and a retired accountant in Saltcoats, and who has spent countless thousand hours in the church's service, has argued that buildings must be drastically reduced because the church is strapped for cash. Those congregations which have carried the burden of the others are finding it less and less easy to do so, and the sale of buildings is the only possible way to raise money, without which the church will be unable to function.

Findlay's argument, which he makes very persuasively, has never convinced me for two reasons. First of all it assumes that congregations who have been denied a minister and deprived of a building will continue to support the Church of Scotland at the rate they did when they had a minister and a building, and I think that is unrealistic. But, secondly, even if their buildings were sold, and realised a capital sum, at the present costs of paying ordained ministers or ancillary workers, the sum realised would not last very long. The crisis would only be postponed and in doing do valuable assets usable by communities would have been lost. And at today's rates of interest the income will not go very far.

Another typical response is administrative reorganisation. A number of Councils have been formed with constituent committees. The representation which presbyteries used to have on the Boards and committees has been abolished, making promised savings in travel and expenses. And a Council of Assembly has been set up to be a co-ordinating body with executive responsibility over the church's administration, and the power to establish for the church what spending should have priority at a time of financial restraint.

There has long been a need for a body which is capable of taking executive decisions in the Church, and I see nothing inherently wrong with that, so long as the executive is answerable to the General Assembly and its actions are transparent. It is early days to assess a reorganisation that in some ways still needs to bed down. In that the minutes of the Council of Assembly are available for inspection on the Church of Scotland's website, there seems to be an attempt to make the Council's proceedings more transparent. The Council has certainly struck a blow or two at some of the traditional power-bases in the Church. But there is also evidence that its existence has encouraged a "bunker" mentality amongst those who sense that their traditionally entrenched position is being undermined. For a long time the Church has lacked any mechanism to prioritise its work and so establish budgetary priorities. The constant cry has gone up every time some area of work has been cut back that the Church cannot abandon this work or it will be denying its true function. But that is simply rhetoric. The fact is that the Church has not engaged in real budgeting, as it would be recognised in any commercial enterprise. It has simply estimated how much can be expected to come into its coffers and divided that up.

Structural reorganisation, however desirable, seldom halts institutional decline; it merely diverts attention from it!

A third response of institutions under threat is to require everyone to be "on message", to minimise dissent and to stress the virtuous necessity of singing from the same hymn sheet. Those who represent the Church, but most especially the moderator, are expected to "talk up the Church". Thus, when Andrew McLellan was moderator and floated an idea, in the sermon at the opening of the Assembly in 2000, that a journalist should be encouraged to write a book about the Church of Scotland, and subsequently Harry Reid produced *Outside Verdict* there was suspicion of the project, rubbishing of the result and the decision that what was effectively a rejoinder to Harry – by Principal Clerk Finlay Macdonald, *Confidence in a Changing Church* – should be published.

I found myself an unexpected witness of the tendency to strengthening central control shortly after Harry's book was published. He and I were invited by the Church's magazine *Life and Work* to debate the future of the Church at a lunchtime event at the Scottish Christian Resources Exhibition at Ingliston. A little earlier there had been pressure put on the previous Editor of *Life and Work* to pulp an entire edition of the magazine. On the day before Harry and I were to debate, I was contacted by *Life and Work* to let me know that someone from the fourth floor of the Church's offices had insisted on taking part in the debate "to make sure that the official view of the Church was represented".

I hope I am right in attributing the tightening of the church's bureaucracy's grip to an anxious determination of those who are employed to plan long-term strategy to ensure that their strategy is implemented. There is, of course, another interpretation: that of people with power wanting to protect it. Christians, of all people, should be very suspicious of those with power: because they should be very suspicious of themselves. We are all sinners and all of us are likely to misuse what power we have. And those who have power in the church, and who ritually deny that they do, are as susceptible as anyone else to the temptation to abuse it.

Just as I was beginning my ministry, one of my old teachers, Ian Henderson, published a book called *Power without Glory*. I wouldn't use his language, which in today's church would be regarded as sexist, but it was fairly common language then. I would, however, endorse what he says about power and the church: he writes that anyone who argues in church circles "that there is such a thing as a will to power among ecclesiastics is soon aware that he has said the wrong thing. Yet how foolish to pretend that it is not there. For all churchmen by virtue of the very commission laid upon them to bring God to men are specially exposed to the temptation to give divine significance to what is all too human in their lives. A Catholic priest can turn cheap wine into the blood of Christ, the Protestant minister at the end of some vapid and ill-prepared discourse can say 'May the Lord add his blessing to the preaching of His Word'. Are not all of us, who are ordained to bring the Gospel of Christ to men not especially exposed to the temptation of saying however unconsciously 'Le bon Dieu, s'est moi' and going on to canonise our thoughts, our prejudices, and our actions, our neuroses and our imperialistic drives?"

Those who don't recognise the truth of that are deluding themselves.

7

"Minister's marriage on rocks" read the headline in *The Glasgow Herald* on the last Saturday of September in 1986, informing readers of what our families and the congregation of Paisley Abbey had known for two months, that Heather and I had separated after twenty-one years together.

On the first Sunday of August, I read to a meeting of elders a statement which Heather and I had agreed. It said that during the summer we had accepted what she had known for a long time, that she did not want her future to be with me, and that as a result we had decided to separate. Before I spoke to the elders, I gave the Clerk of Paisley presbytery a frank outline of what had led up to this decision. Shortly afterwards, I spoke to my closest friends in the presbytery, Tom McWilliam (who happened to be moderator of presbytery at the time) and Douglas Alexander (who had supervised Heather's probationary year after she had completed her training to be a minister). In the twelve months that followed I could not have survived without their support, and the support of Pat McWilliam and Joyce Alexander, because, after an initial eerie period, the next few months were to be hellish. Nor could I have survived without the support of Irene and Martin Doole, my two closest friends outside the ministry. Allegations about what had broken up the marriage were made, and although the allegations had no foundation, I had little stomach to continue as a minister when I was the object of this sort of campaign. I decided that I would quietly resign as minister of Paisley Abbey, demit my status as a minister, and see what the future held. On a speaking engagement in Edinburgh for one of my oldest friends, Andrew McLellan, I explained what had happened since the separation and my decision to leave the Abbey.

It is never easy to be a minister to a friend. A friend is close but a minister has to be objective and the two can run counter to each other. While always making it clear that our friendship was not at stake, Andrew asked for honest answers. We talked for a long time, and then he said what I should have realised from the start: that instead of creeping away from it all into the shadows, I should say to the presbytery Clerk, in today's language, that those who thought they had a complaint to make should make it formally, in ecclesiastical language raise a "fama" against me, or abandon their complaint. I had no great wish to defend myself on the floor of the presbytery, but I agreed to ask the presbytery Clerk to ask for a formal complain in the form of a "fama" or an end to the complaints.

As I was talking to the presbytery Clerk, Heather was returning from eight weeks in Israel, where she was studying on a scholarship she had been given. Her absence, naturally, allowed those who wanted to make two and two add up to five assume that my account of events was false. She was not there to contradict it. However, on the Sunday after the presbytery Clerk had told the representatives of a group of detractors that the presbytery would only consider its complaint if it was formally framed as a "fama", with supporting evidence, Heather turned up in Paisley Abbey, took her usual seat and appeared on perfectly good terms with me. I was told shortly afterwards that there were several very embarrassed, ashen faces when she was seen taking her pew.

After we separated, and subsequently divorced, Heather pursued the academic career which she was always drawn to, and married a professor of biblical studies. Our two boys, Kevin and Robert, graduated from Strathclyde and Glasgow Universities respectively. Kevin works in the music industry in London with his partner Gill, and Robert is a university teacher of English, married to Gayle. The friendship which I had with a member of Paisley Abbey, Evelyn Christie, developed and we were married in 1989. Our daughter Carolyn, known to everyone as Cally, was born the following year. To both of them I owe more than I can ever repay. Evelyn picked me up from despair and gave me hope, Cally took that hope and gave it a new form.

However much I wanted to stay on in Paisley Abbey, and two days a week I really did, I couldn't handle continuing being minister there for much longer. Each Sunday in Advent in 1986 there were services broadcast from the Abbey, which I conducted, and at which the preacher was the recently appointed Bishop of Edinburgh, Richard Holloway. The services were recorded on two weekday evenings, and on the evening of one of the recordings, Richard strolled into the Abbey vestry and sat down.

"There's a vacancy in religious broadcasting at the BBC" he said. "You must apply for it". So I did. I was interviewed in April 1987 and the following Sunday announced to the congregation that I would be leaving at the end of June.

For a year before I joined the staff of the Religious Broadcasting Department in Scotland I had been involved, to a limited extent, in radio production. Ian Mackenzie, who was head of the department, asked me to devise a format which would give the traditional church service one last chance to prove it should be the main basis of religious broadcasting in radio. Since church services then consisted mainly of music and preaching, I proposed that every Sunday for a year there should be a service, from a very limited number of locations, where the standard of music was high, and whose ministers would agree to lead the service, but would allow the BBC to invite the ablest preachers (from a wide range of denominations) to the pulpit. Each service would follow a similar pattern. Three locations were chosen: Paisley Abbey, New Kilpatrick and Dunblane Cathedral. The services would be recorded with clergy and choir but no congregation, partly for reasons of cost (two services were recorded in each evening session) and partly to ensure as high as possible a standard of hymns and anthems.

By the time the series ended, I was myself a radio producer and able to reflect from a different perspective on why the series failed to breathe life into the traditionally broadcast church service.

Undoubtedly the proposal itself was flawed because in drawing it up I failed to take account of two things. The first was the fact that the audience for broadcast worship was predominantly if not entirely made up of people who were churchgoers themselves, and the trend was towards informality, modern songs rather than traditional hymns. Services conducted from places where worship followed a traditional liturgical pattern seemed staid and old-fashioned to an audience increasingly accustomed to something very different. The second flaw in the reasoning behind the series appears paradoxically to contradict the first. It was that although fine preachers were used, the sort of preaching which an important part of the audience wanted was the preaching of a former age, literary, rounded, rhetorical. This was the expectation of that part of the audience which could no longer attend church and so their experience of active participation in worship had stopped before the increasing trend to informality and the devaluing of preaching generally had taken hold.

So that year-long series called "The Word" was seriously flawed in failing to take account of the existing audience for broadcast church services, part of which was accustomed to a very different style worship, and part of which expected a very different style of preaching.

By the time the series ended, I had already come to the conclusion that there were two equally serious flaws in any broadcast of a church service *as a piece of radio*. The first is that radio is an intimate medium and church services (even of the more informal sort) are designed for large buildings where voices need to be heard. The second, much more serious flaw was that the number of people who were able to make the imaginative leap from their kitchen or car to a church and relate to what was happening was diminishing at a very fast rate.

Church services were a wholly appropriate form of religious broadcasting in the days when churchgoing was at its peak in Scotland. But those days were gone. If religious broadcasting tied itself to a style to which fewer people could relate, then it would eventually wither and die. Ian Mackenzie took little persuading that this was the case. Ever since he had taken charge of the department he had been attempting to widen the audience for religious broadcasting on television. With the support of first the Acting Controller of BBC Scotland, Pat Walker, and the Controller, Alastair Hetherington, his policy was to look for a wider audience than worship attracted. In his book *Inside BBC Scotland,* Hetherington takes up the story.

This policy, he says, went down very badly with the Church of Scotland. "A cry grew up: why the loss of church services? Was the BBC abandoning them? The Church was already aware that it faced a reduction in numbers and influence. They now felt betrayed by Ian Mackenzie. There were a number of letters to Queen Margaret Drive, and there was another factor which Mackenzie did not know in any detail at the time. A campaign against BBC Scotland's religious policy came to life, encouraged sad to say by the man who for many years, until 1972, had been the BBC's Head of Religion. He was Ronald Falconer, a man of justifiably high reputation, and in the past a friend and supporter of Mackenzie. It was not helpful that, from his position as Convener of the Church of Scotland's publicity committee, he orchestrated opposition to Mackenzie's strategy. When someone of Falconer's standing said of Mackenzie: 'This man is ruining it all', why should Church ministers disbelieve him?

Ian Mackenzie, however, had a straight response. 'The only thing – deliver the goods.' He was not going to back-track. The critics, given time, would see the sense of his efforts to reach a much wider audience (as later most of them did)."

By the time I joined the BBC staff, Ian Mackenzie had won the battle in television, but radio had been guided for nearly twenty years by Douglas Aitken, who had been appointed by Ronald Falconer, and who found it difficult to step outside the parameters he inherited from Falconer, who I recall once saying to the General Assembly of the Church of Scotland "The BBC's Religious Broadcasting Department is the broadcasting arm of the Church".

Just as I was getting settled in to the BBC job, a new Head of Radio was appointed. I had known Neil Fraser since we were at university together. Ian Mackenzie and I set out to persuade him that the change which Ian had overseen in television now needed to be pushed through in radio. It was time, yet again, to face a battle with the Church over the loss of broadcast church services. And the strategy had to be the same: deliver the goods.

Along with Mo McCullough, who was a Production Assistant with the department when I joined but soon became first an Assistant Producer and later a Producer, we devised a strategy which involved making programmes, which were based either in studios or on location – the arrival of the compact professional recording machine made location recording by a producer so much easier and cheaper – and which could be used by a person of faith as an aid to spiritual reflection or meditation but could also be listened to by a much wider audience. I believed (and have become increasingly convinced) that a sense of spirituality is by no means confined to those who claim a formal connection with some form of institutional religion.

There were letters of complaint sent to BBC Scotland's Controller and Head of Radio. There were critical motions passed by presbyteries. There were questions asked and complaints aired in the General Assembly. I was asked by more than one kirk session to explain myself, and on these occasions took rueful comfort from the words of the late Professor William Barclay: "If you are given the choice of being thrown to a den of lions or a den of Christians, choose the lions!"

Ian Mackenzie's successor as Head of Religious Broadcasting (a post for which at the time I applied but I now realise it was my huge good fortune not to have succeeded in getting) would have put the clock back had he lasted more than a few months in the job. However the policy began to deliver the goods.

Two straws in the wind convinced me we were on the right lines. Someone I knew slightly contacted me after a Sunday morning programme. He wanted to tell me how much he had enjoyed it and how much it had meant to him. "To be honest" he said, "I didn't know it was a religious programme until I heard your name announced at the end as the producer."

When I told that story to one of the kirk sessions, which had asked me to explain myself to them, there was an immediate outcry. "You see," I was told, "you're making programmes that aren't recognisably religious". I, on the other hand, took it as a compliment that we were enticing as listeners people who did not think of themselves as conventionally religious and who would have reached for the off-switch at the first organ chords of a church service.

The other encouraging moment came at Easter 1988, when the radio reviewer of *The Scotsman* began her column "Only an ostrich could have failed to notice the transformation in Radio Scotland's Religious Broadcasting in recent months", and went on accurately to interpret what we were trying to do, and to praise a number of our efforts.

For several years, Mo McCullough and I were responsible for forty-five minutes of broadcasting every Sunday on Radio Scotland, as well as extra programmes at Christmas and Easter and additional series and programmes which were broadcast through the week. We produced *Thought for the Day* every weekday of the year. As well as the Radio Scotland output, we had to deliver at least eight live church services for Radio 4, an equal number of recorded *Sunday Half Hour* programmes for Radio 2, and at least a couple of transmissions of *Choral Evensong* for Radio 3. We made documentaries for Radio 4 and features for Radio 3. We were ludicrously busy and grossly under-staffed. The trouble was that when we tried to explain to the management of BBC Scotland that we were overstretched and needed extra resources because of commitment to Radios 2, 3 and 4 we were told that network stations were contributing nothing to our salaries and so had no claim on us; and when we tried to persuade the networks to fund more production assistance we were informed that it was BBC Scotland's decision to axe posts and we would have to live with the consequences. An output which five years or so earlier had been produced by four producers, a researcher and three production assistants was being sustained by Mo and myself and a single production assistant. We had, however, enjoyed ourselves thoroughly

James Boyle, when he was Head of Radio, Scotland once said that religious broadcasting had established itself as an essential part of the structure of BBC radio in Scotland "and not" he added "something which pops in from time to time from a portacabin and then disappears again". On the way to achieving that, the part which Mo McCullough played will probably go largely unsung, but it should not go unrecognised. The award – of a Sanford St Martin prize, for one of her programmes in the brilliant series *The Eternal Blue,* exactly the sort of programme we had set out to show many years earlier, that should be the benchmark for religious broadcasting – probably gave me more pride than it gave her.

Improbably, perhaps, the other person to whom we owe the expansion of religious broadcasting and the growth of the radio department is John Birt, and his policy of ensuring that the BBC knew the financial cost of absolutely everything; and coupled with the name of John Birt must go the name of Andrew Barr.

If ever there was a case of the right man at the right time it was Andrew's arrival as Head of Religious Broadcasting in May 1990.

The Birt era was about to begin. Although it was a disastrous period for the BBC as a whole, with armies of accountants and business managers swarming everywhere, and initiative and creativity stifled, for religious broadcasting in BBC Scotland one of John Birt's demands was good news, though it took me a little time to understand that.

Shortly after he took up his post, Andrew Barr asked me to work out (for the accountants!) how much production time it took for every one of the programmes for which I was responsible. I went off and spent a couple of days coming up with an answer, but when I took the figures to him he just laughed. "No, Johnston, this is how long you and Mo take just now, working far longer than you should. What we want is what it is reasonable to expect a producer to spend on each programme." I went off and did the sums again, and of course realised that we needed another couple of members of staff at least. Since John Birt had decreed that everything done within the BBC had to be paid for by somebody, money from the programmes we produced for network came into the department, as well as money for the programmes we produced for Radio Scotland. Suddenly we could afford to take on new members of staff and we had the money to pay for them. Immediately the department began to expand to meet the work we had.

Credit, however, must go to Andrew Barr, who had come back to BBC Scotland. He had worked in television here in the sixties. His career took him to be Deputy Head of Religious Broadcasting for the BBC in London, and then Head of Religious programmes for TVS, the independent television company covering a large part of the south of England. He was a television producer with a proven track record in making innovative religious television programmes. He immediately recognised how the financial reforms being introduced by John Birt could be made to work for us and he made sure that I learned lessons he had learned in the much harsher world of commercial television. Looking back, had things been different, and had I succeeded in taking charge of the department when Ian Mackenzie retired, I would never have been able to grasp with anything like the assurance of Andrew the implications for us of the Birt revolution. All of us in religious broadcasting in BBC Scotland owe him an enormous debt. I still enjoy a quiet smile when I recall the early days of John Birt's time as Director General. People in other departments, and also many in the religious broadcasting department, then in London, were moaning about having to learn business methods, and complaining about having to pay for the use of studios or get permission from a business manager to purchase a new recording machine, while we in Scotland were streets ahead, making the new system work to our advantage.

John Birt's demand for total costing immediately benefited a department like ours which was very small and had been historically under-staffed, whereas departments which had been traditionally well cared for suddenly began to discover that they could not afford to maintain the levels of staffing and there had to be cut-backs.

Then a new Head of Radio in Scotland, James Boyle (dubbed by the media, MacBirt) completely transformed Radio Scotland's schedule and outlook. James was and is a very cautious man. He spends a long time taking everything in before he commits himself to a policy or a course of action. When he does, he can be ruthless in ensuring that it is carried out. In my experience he very rarely gets it wrong, and it was a tribute to him when Radio Scotland was made the Sony Station of the year.

It was at least six months after he had become Head of Radio that James Boyle asked me what I would do if he gave religious broadcasting three hours to fill on a Sunday morning from 7.00 am until 10.00 am. Until then we had produced forty five minutes of programmes from 9.30 am until 10.15 am, following a news and newspaper review programme at 9.00 am. James' hunch was that in Scotland (he rightly took a very different view when he became controller of Radio 4) nobody really wanted heavy news analysis before about 10.00 am on a Sunday morning. So I was asked to draw up a scheme and to tell him how much it would cost in total. The result was the *Sunday Morning* sequence which began at 7.00 am with a very gentle programme of words and music presented by Georgie Baxendale, which led into a twenty minute programme about voluntary work going on around the country. After the eight o'clock news, the *Greetings* programme – which has been part of the Radio Scotland furniture for decades, and presented, I remember, by the legendary Howard M Lockhart (of blessed memory) – was presented by Ian Aldred, who linked all the three hours together. After the nine o'clock news there was a reflective, meditative feature and the sequence ended with a religious news and views magazine which we called *Benchmark*.

Since then there have been various amendments and changes.

Colin Mackay took over the presentation of the three hours, and Father John Fitzsimmons became the presenter of the Greetings Programme.

John Fitzsimmons is a Roman Catholic priest who had become one of my closest friends. He had been Rector of the Scots College in Rome before he was asked to return home because his scholarship was too much for the Roman Catholic hierarchy to cope with. He is, without doubt, the best bishop the Roman Catholic Church never had, and I have valued his support and friendship more than I can record.

However, when I asked John Fitzsimmons to present the

Greetings programme, it was not because of his ecclesiastical pedigree or personal friendship but because I knew that, hidden behind the fifteen languages he spoke and the theological brain he possessed, there was an encyclopaedic knowledge of popular music. He still broadcasts to a huge audience.

The listening figures for the three hours were always high, and, at least as important even in a post Birtian BBC, the cost per listener (an important index) has always been low.

The increase in the department allowed me to offer more feature programmes for James Boyle's weekday schedule, and two series in particular he had no hesitation in commissioning: one on figures in the history of the Scottish Church who were *Right at the Wrong Time* and one on the New Testament, *It Ain't Necessarily So.* When the latter was transmitted, a Roman Catholic bishop commented that, of course, he was well aware of the scholarly views which the series attempted to explore but had we considered the effect it might have on lay people whose faith might be disturbed by being told that not everything in the gospels was actually said by Jesus? This was the sort of attitude which made someone like James Boyle very angry, and it made me very sad, for whether as a parish minister or as a religious broadcaster I had always believed that congregations or audiences were adults who were entitled to the total honesty of a preacher or a producer.

One summer in the mid 1990s, we decided to run a series of eight twenty minute "filler" programmes which could be recorded well in advance and so allow for staff holidays. In each programme a guest would be asked to choose two pieces of writing and two pieces of music and talk to me about them and about their life. The eight week run continued until 2005, and the length of the programme was extended to half an hour. Writing in *The Herald*, radio critic Ann Donald wrote of the programme, "Tucked away in the early morning slot on Radio Scotland is McKay's show, *Personal Touch.* His innocuous-sounding programme slices through weekday waffle and japes to prod and poke personal revelations from well-kent names … Rustling under McKay's pleasant exterior is a zealous missionary of the truth, relaxed enough to let his subjects talk themselves into a tight corner". It was the nicest thing anyone had said about me since a colleague told someone who was coming to be my assistant at Paisley Abbey that Johnston McKay is not a bastard, but it will take you three months to find that out!

8

In a broadcasting career of over thirty years there has only been one terrifying moment. It came as something of a surprise in 1992 when it was announced that the national service to mark the end of the Gulf War would be held in Glasgow Cathedral. When the Falklands War ended, the national service had been held in St Paul's Cathedral and the Archbishop of Canterbury, Robert Runcie had preached. But Glasgow's lovely cathedral was to play host to the entire government and the top brass of the armed forces, and the Queen and the Duke of Edinburgh were to be present. The service was due to start at eleven o'clock and by early morning I was with the outside broadcast vans in a street below the Cathedral's east wall. The service was being televised, with commentary by Tom Fleming, and so there was the usual large presence of television vans. I had a radio outside broadcast van which contained all the production and transmitting equipment, and the van providing a studio for the radio commentator was twenty yards or so down the road. The radio commentator was Andrew McLellan.

Exactly on time at five minutes to eleven o'clock we went on air on both Radio Scotland and Radio 4. By eleven o'clock there was no sign of the royal car. The royal train had broken down outside Motherwell and the Queen was going to be about forty minutes late. However although this information was relayed to the television production team they did not think to pass it on to their radio colleagues, and so we continued to broadcast thinking that at any moment the Queen would appear. After ten minutes or so, Andrew had exhausted every piece of information that he had to share with the listeners. For long periods they simply heard the organ playing. At one point, after twenty minutes, I remember running along to the van which served as a studio, and handing Andrew a copy of the guidebook to Glasgow Cathedral, with a note suggesting that he just read great chunks of it, and when he stopped, we would fade up the organ while he found another bit of the book to read. Eventually, forty minutes late, the Queen arrived and the service began. I cannot remember what princely sum we paid to Andrew for commentating that day but, whatever it was, he deserved ten times as much!

If Glasgow Cathedral was the venue for my most terrifying broadcasting moment, it was also the venue for one of the saddest, when Donald Dewar's funeral took place there in October 2000.

On the evening he was taken into hospital I telephoned my cousin Kenneth Munro, who was one of Donald's closest friends. Kenneth told me that Donald was on a life-support system, being kept alive until his daughter could reach him from her home in Brussels. Andrew McLellan, who had commentated on the Gulf War Service, was, by then, moderator of the General Assembly. He was, and is, one of my closest friends. As soon as I heard how seriously ill Donald was, I phoned Andrew who, with the pastoral insights of a fine parish minister, allied to the sensitive antennae of the Kirk's official spokesman, immediately went to Edinburgh's Western Infirmary and spent some time alongside Donald with his family. The following day, having contributed to *Thought for the Day*, I contacted my old friend Douglas Alexander, whose daughter Wendy had been one of Donald's most important aides and, of course a member of his Scottish Executive. Not entirely to my surprise, Douglas told me that he had been asked to conduct Donald's funeral, and that he would keep in touch with me about arrangements, so that I could brief BBC Scotland's senior management.

The following day Douglas phoned me to say that there was some debate about where the funeral should take place. Some wanted it to be held in Donald's constituency, and there was talk of it taking place in one of the churches at Knightswood Cross, which was close to several other churches which could host relays. Others were holding out for Glasgow Cathedral. There was even talk of St Giles' Cathedral in Edinburgh, but I could not imagine the funeral of someone so quintessentially Glaswegian and egalitarian taking place in St Giles'. Eventually I was told that the service would be held in Glasgow Cathedral, and that it would be conducted by Douglas Alexander. So that evening I was a little surprised to hear the minister of Glasgow Cathedral, Dr Bill Morris, say on television how pleased he was that he had been asked to conduct Donald's funeral service.

This was just the first of many hiccups that were to take place. The Labour Party, who were strangers to ecclesiastical protocol, thought that asking for the use of Glasgow Cathedral meant just that – the use of a public building. Dr Morris, on being asked if the funeral could take place in Glasgow Cathedral, naturally assumed that as minister he was being asked to conduct it.

These niceties were soon resolved, and it was announced that Douglas Alexander would conduct the funeral. An order of service was drawn up, and by the Saturday after Donald died the main parts of the service were agreed. While Douglas would conduct the service, the moderator and one of the parish priests from Donald's constituency would say prayers, Tony Blair would read from the bible and Donald's close associate, David Whitton, would read from the bible and the works of R.H. Tawney (the latter a passage Donald had chosen when he was a guest on *Personal Touch*), and tributes would be paid by the journalist Ruth Wishart and the Chancellor of the Exchequer, Gordon Brown.

It was proposed that, once the service was over, the organist should play a medley comprising *A Man's A Man For A' That, The Red Flag* and *L'Internazionale*. Douglas Alexander told me that the organist of Glasgow Cathedral had, perhaps not surprisingly, refused to play any of these tunes. I began to wonder whether it might be appropriate for me, as the BBC producer involved, to commission someone to compose a medley of these tunes for a small instrumental group to play. It was suggested to me that perhaps the combination of Aly Bain and Phil Cunningham might be the right combination. I tracked Phil Cunningham down to a theatre in either Bournemouth or Brighton. He contacted Aly. By the Saturday evening I was able to assure Douglas Alexander that Aly and Phil would play.

On the Wednesday of the following week Donald's funeral took place. I was the radio commentator, and sat in a van very close to the spot where Andrew McLellan had talked at great length before the start of the Gulf War service. I described quietly what was happening as the funeral service began and occasionally introduced who was to speak next during the service. However, when the funeral was over, and as Donald's coffin emerged into the nave of the Cathedral, and Aly and Phil started playing, I found words difficult to say. I struggled until I described the coffin emerging into the sunlight, and then, with the fiddle and accordion still playing in the background, tears took over.

Later that evening, after he had conducted a private service for the family at Knightswood Crematorium, Douglas Alexander and his wife Joyce joined Evelyn, Carolyn and myself for dinner at Gleddoch House. It was a riotous occasion.

It was fortunate, both for the Church and the BBC, that Andrew McLellan was moderator at the time of Donald's death, because both owed a lot to his sensitivity and insight. However, the BBC has not always found moderators as sympathetic as Andrew.

I should, perhaps, declare an interest, in that the very first of the programmes reflecting the new policy for religious broadcasting on radio which I promoted was presented by Andrew McLellan. Over the years he has been a brilliant contributor to *Thought for the Day*, a regular writer of scripts, a commentator – not just at the Gulf Service but at the Lockerbie Memorial Service – and my successor as a presenter of radio coverage of the General Assembly, so I am, perhaps, biased. However he did not always deliver the goods. When, a few years ago, I discovered that he had never been to what the sentimental call "the Holy Land" and the politically correct call "Israel/Palestine", I decided to take him there with some other broadcasters and record his immediate reactions to seeing places associated with the life of Jesus. We went first to Nazareth, and drove up the steep, twisting road to the grounds of a hotel, from which we overlooked the town. I asked Andrew if he was ready to give me his first reactions. He asked for a moment or two to gather his thoughts, so I fiddled with the tape recorder and made sure the microphone was live and then he said he was ready. I waited for his first insight into the place Jesus knew as his home town. "I'm standing high above Nazareth" he said, "and it just looks like Kilmarnock"!

Each year the moderator of the General Assembly is invited to pay an official visit to BBC Scotland. Some of them are hilarious. Some of them made me sad.

The most hilarious was the visit paid by Dr Fraser McLuskey, when he was moderator. At the time I chaired the BBC's Religious Advisory committee and was invited to join BBC big-wigs for dinner at the end of the moderator's day long visit. I arrived, as bidden, about seven o'clock in the evening and was shown up to the office of the Controller of the time, Pat Chalmers, whom I found laughing hysterically along with the then Head of Radio, Stan Taylor. I asked what was amusing them so much. They told me that earlier in the day, after coffee, they had taken the moderator on a tour of Broadcasting House. The moderator was dressed in his full finery – court dress, breeches, and lace ruffles at the wrist and neck. As arranged, they had visited a television studio where, as it happened a programme was being made about Dr Johnson's companion James Boswell. As the moderator was ushered into the studio in full gear, the floor manager shouted. "You're ***** late: get over there!" He mistook the moderator for an extra!

Much more serious was a visit paid by a later moderator. He had been on a morning's tour of the building, where he had not exactly ingratiated himself with some senior female executives and producers, whom he insisted in addressing as "love" and "dear". The Religious Broadcasting Department was summoned to meet him for an official lunch, at which, even before we had cut into the first course of melon and parma ham, BBC Scotland's Controller John McCormick announced that as the moderator was a very busy man he did not like to waste time, and so he wanted to start a conversation right away. John McCormick said, with the graciousness which is a hallmark of his style, that the BBC was extremely grateful to the moderator for spending some time with us, and that at a time when the BBC's charter was being renewed, it was important that important people such as the moderator had every opportunity to put questions to the BBC.

So without even touching his melon and parma ham the moderator embarked on a series of questions which became more embarrassing as course succeeded course.

We were all slightly mystified when he began by explaining that he had been brought up in the days when a product like Bovril had been regarded as wholesome and healthy; but he had been very surprised recently to see an advert on television in which a young man was leaving home, clearly to set up home with his girl friend, and that the purpose of the advert was to commend Bovril. The healthy and wholesome commended through a young man obviously intending to live *in sin*.

The Controller cleared his throat, coughed a little, and said, somewhat nervously, that this was a very important point which the moderator had raised, but perhaps it might be better addressed to the Independent Television Authority which was responsible for advertising on ITV.

"Is there perhaps anything more specific to the BBC which the moderator would like to ask?" the Controller said.

"Why is the moderator not invited to take part in the British Legion's Festival of Remembrance in the Albert Hall?" he asked, and went on to say that he had to insist that as moderator he receive an invitation along with Anglican and Roman Catholic dignitaries to the Festival of Remembrance, the previous weekend.

At this point around the table the BBC representatives concentrated on their plates, and the church representatives who accompanied the moderator looked a trifle sheepish.

BBC Scotland's Controller, who had not been Secretary to the Board of Governors in London without learning a diplomatic skill or two, explained that the Festival of Remembrance was entirely run by the Royal British Legion and the BBC simply broadcast what happened in the Albert Hall, but had no responsibility for the evening's content. Was there anything else the moderator wanted to ask, perhaps touching on the BBC's charter renewal or its future plans?

Well since future plans had been mentioned, the moderator did have something to ask. He believed that the BBC was committed to reflecting the religious diversity of the country. However, he demanded pointedly "Do you recognise that this is still a Christian country, and that other faiths are tolerated, but no more than tolerated here?"

I thought the senior executive sitting opposite me was going to explode, as the Controller gently explained that people of whatever religious persuasion paid a licence fee and were entitled to have their faiths respected and included in programmes.

"I have a final question," said the moderator, "and in many ways it is the most serious."

Having heard his previous questions we all held our

breath.

"Why have I never seen a hospital chaplain on *Casualty?*"

At this point the Controller caught my eye and I recognised an appealing look such as Walter Scott's Jeannie Deans might have made in the direction of the Queen when she was pleading for the life of her sister. I was meant to mount a rescue mission.

"I don't normally watch *Casualty*" I said. "But last Saturday night, knowing that the moderator was to be on the Festival of Remembrance, I switched on *Casualty* just before it. And there was a chaplain on last week's programme."

The moderator sat down, with nothing more to say. I knew he could not possibly have seen that episode of *Casualty* since he was in the Albert Hall. I had not seen the episode either!

The Roman Catholic hierarchy provided as much light relief, but seldom in such official settings. On one occasion I had to go to make a programme with Cardinal Winning in his offices in Clyde Street, where a custom-built studio had been built by a sometime BBC colleague, Father Willie McDade. We knew that the Cardinal was attending a funeral and so might be late for the interview, but we arrived in very good time, and were shown into the studio (from which, as it happens, several years later, the radio commentary on the Cardinal's funeral mass was to be broadcast.) As is usual there was a technical cubicle and beyond it a studio. However none of us from the BBC could find the switch to power up either the cubicle or the studio. BBC technical staff find it a bit embarrassing if they are not able even to switch on the power. For at least half an hour we searched everywhere but to no avail. Eventually the Cardinal arrived and we told him the problem "This is ridiculous" he said, and went off to find someone who might know where the power switch was. But neither his communications officer, nor his secretary, nor his personal assistant, were able to help. Eventually a wee man appeared who said he knew all about it.

"You see" he said to the Cardinal confidentially "Willie McDade designed this studio, and he didn't want the wrong people using it, so there isn't a power switch. You just do this…" and the wee man reached out towards a fuse box, opened it, and put the fuse back in place. And behold there was light and power!

I will remember the subsequent broadcast, because it revealed that however much a prince of the church Tom Winning was, and however distinguished as a canon lawyer, his grasp of the New Testament was far from sure. He was talking about the events of Holy Week, and at one point he said "One of Jesus' disciples even took a sword and tried to cut off somebody's ear" and then he turned towards me and said "I can't remember which one of the disciples it was, but it was one of them". I whispered quietly "Peter, Cardinal, Peter"!

By the time Tom Winning died, Andrew Barr had retired, and I was responsible for both television and radio religious broadcasting. The morning following his death I was contacted and told that the arrangements for the coverage of the Cardinal's funeral would be in the hands of the News and Current Affairs Department but that we would be expected to share in the planning and production. This had been the arrangement for Donald Dewar's funeral, and since that was as much, if not more, of a political than a religious event I had agreed to it. But the funeral of a Cardinal was a different matter. I explained that I realised that there was great public interest in Cardinal Winning, and that his high profile had meant that News and Current Affairs regarded him almost as their property. However, I said, his funeral mass was a religious occasion, and if the coverage of the funeral mass was not entirely in the hands of religious broadcasting, I would regard that as a massive vote of no confidence and would have to consider whether I should resign.

Shortly afterwards the Controller asked to see me. He wanted to know why I was being so awkward, why I was engaging in what he called "turf wars" with News and Current Affairs.

I have known John McCormick for over twenty years and I like him enormously. However I knew that I could not say what he really wanted to hear: that it had all been a misunderstanding and everything would be fine. He gave me the one opportunity I needed when he said "Tell me. What added value will Religious Broadcasting bring to our coverage of the funeral if you are in charge if it?" I said that we would turn coverage of an event into a religious television programme. He said he would get in touch with me when he had made a decision. Half an hour later he phoned with his decision: "News and Current Affairs are producing coverage until the procession enters the Cathedral. After that, it's over to you."

I was relieved, not least because I had not told Evelyn that by the end of the day I might not have a job!

That afternoon I sat down with Anne Muir, who was a hugely talented television producer and director. Since neither of us is a Roman Catholic we needed to discuss how to do what I had promised we would: turn the coverage of an event into a television programme. We decided to consult a colleague, who is a very devout Roman Catholic, and ask him what people at the Cardinal's Funeral Mass would be thinking as they waited to receive communion. We were told that they would be thinking how what they were doing, taking communion, would be in Tom Winning's favour in the world beyond.

It was not Anne's theology nor mine, and Anne said she would go away and think about how what had been described could be reflected on television. There were obviously going to be long parts, of what would be a very long service, when it might be right to show footage of the Cardinal, but it would seem odd in the least to see one shot of the Cardinal's coffin and another of him animatedly active on film.

The following morning, when I met Anne, she had hit on a

brilliant idea. Any footage of the Cardinal which belonged to his life which was ended would be indicated by transferring all pictures of the cardinal to black and white and slowing them down. And for specific moments during the mass she planned to superimpose a montage of candles over the footage on the screen. It was brilliant, and led Bishop Joe Devine, in a letter thanking the BBC for its coverage, to mention specifically the sensitive and creative use of images which enabled those watching the BBC's coverage in the six churches around the archdiocese (where screens were set up), or in the street outside the cathedral, to believe their experience of the funeral was better than those who were present in the building.

And so, from one of the most moving experiences of my broadcasting career, to one of the most amusing. It took place before I joined the BBC staff but was presenting coverage of the Kirk's General Assembly from an Edinburgh studio. The plan was that I would introduce extracts recorded earlier from the Assembly's debates, and, every so often discuss them with a guest in the studio.

Suddenly I realised that the studio clock had stopped. I had no idea whether it had just stopped or whether it had stopped some time earlier but it apparently showed there were about five minutes of the programme to go. I introduced the recording of a speech from the Assembly and pressed the talk-back button to the cubicle next door. "The studio clock has stopped and I don't know how long we've got to go" I barked. In the cubicle next door there were two producers, two audio supervisors and a production assistant. After a silence which seemed interminable the producer, Willie McDade, he of the flexible fuse in the Archdiocese of Glasgow's offices, said to me in my headphones "After this tape you have time for two more questions". And, just as I was about to tell him in no uncertain terms that his information was less specific than I required, a wonderful audio supervisor called Ken Stewart said to me "Two questions, Johnston. You know: like what is truth and where is God?"

The BBC enabled me to visit places in the world I could never have expected to visit. I made three visits to Israel/Palestine. Though I was never moved for a solitary moment by what are described as the "holy sites", I was always moved by the plight of the Palestinian people.

One of my visits was with Alison Elliot, then Convener of the Church and Nation committee, and Margaret Macintosh, Convener of the committee's International Relations sub-committee. A report had been prepared for the General Assembly, but neither Alison nor Margaret had ever been to Israel/Palestine so I decided that for the television coverage that year, we would take them there and ask them to relate their report to their first hand experience. The visit sticks in my memory because an interview was arranged with the deputy-head of Hamas, the militant Palestinian organisation, which claimed responsibility for many suicide bombings before and since. For a variety of reasons, I had to conduct the interview. We were taken by an extremely circuitous route to a house in Gaza City. Inside, men were armed. The Hamas leader was icy cold, as I tried to ask him how violence could be justified, repeating again and again that the violence he perpetrated against Israelis was a response to the violence originally perpetrated against his people. The facts I could not dispute. The conclusion, however, left me very frightened for the future of people there. I was very relieved when the interview was ended and we eventually crossed the barrier from Gaza back into Israel.

Early in 1995, John Fitzsimmons, Andrew MacLellan, Georgie Baxendale and I spent a week in the Holy Land making about fourteen radio programmes. Two moments on that visit I will never forget.

John Fitzsimmons, a brilliant wit, and I were walking along the shore of the Sea of Galilee. We came across a notice which we took to be prohibitive of diving "No Jumping", and another which read "No Swimming". As we walked on, John turned to me and said "Johnston, has it ever occurred to you that the good Lord had to walk on the bloody water, because you're not allowed to do anything else"!

We recorded one programme just outside the Church of the Nations, next to the Garden of Gethsemane. I suddenly noticed a sign which read "No Explanations inside the Church", presumably to discourage tourist guides from chattering. I noted it carefully and thought that it would do as a sermon illustration some day. I little knew how important that sign was to be, because just a few weeks later the dreadful massacre at Dunblane happened. I had to do *Prayer for the Day* on Radio 4 and *Thought for the Day* on Radio Scotland the next day and used the illustration in both broadcasts. Then I drove to Dunblane to make arrangements for the radio and television broadcasts we would make from the Cathedral the following Sunday. The minister of Dunblane, Colin Macintosh, had been my assistant in Bellahouston Steven, and he asked me if he could use the illustration in his sermon that Sunday morning. Along with the sermon which James Whyte preached as moderator at the Lockerbie memorial service just a matter of weeks after Pan Am 103 was blown out of the skies, these are the finest sermons I have ever heard.

Along with colleagues Anna Magnusson and Erica Morrison, I went to New York shortly after the Twin Towers were destroyed, on what has become known as 9/11. The scripts I had written and the interviews we did were later published on the first anniversary of the tragedy as a book: *Glimpses of Hope*, and on the first anniversary I was invited to present *Time for Reflection* in the Scottish Parliament.

Less than a hundred yards from where the twin towers of the World Trade Centre stood there is an Episcopal Chapel called St Paul's. It's the oldest public building still in use in

New York. It is where George Washington said his prayers on the night after he was inaugurated president. Before September 11th, it provided a pleasing venue for the lunchtime concerts which entertained the financial community which worked close by.

The priest in charge at St Paul's talks very movingly of making his way from his home in Greenwich Village on the morning of September 12th to see what he could rescue from what he was certain would be the ruins of his chapel. But just as he was passing City Hall, he caught sight of the spire of St Paul's. And when he turned the key in the lock, he found that not even a pane of glass had been broken.

As soon as the building was pronounced structurally safe, the clergy and people of St Paul's mother church, Holy Trinity Wall Street began to provide water and hot dogs on the pavement outside the chapel for the rescue workers. The stall was shut down several times a day by the city health authorities; as soon as they left the hot-dog stall resumed. Soon the manager of a restaurant was recruited to help them around the regulations, and the stall moved first onto the porch of the chapel and then inside. An offer was made by the top chefs of the New York hotels to cook extra food in their restaurants and send it down to St Paul's. The morning I was there, breakfast had come from the Waldorf Astoria. Chiropodists volunteered to care for tired feet and so a podiatry clinic was set up in the pew where George Washington worshipped. Beds were provided so that firemen, physically and emotionally exhausted, could snatch a couple of hour's sleep before resuming their searches. Thousand of pairs of gloves were donated and hands which were cut tearing at concrete were protected. Priests were on hand for conversations. And stories were told and listened to by the thousands of volunteers who came in to help, and worked twelve hour shifts round the clock.

On the day I visited, the eucharist was celebrated at the

altar, but everything else continued: In the side aisle men slept. Sausages and scrambled eggs were being served at the back of the church. In George Washington's pew, feet were being washed. On walkie-talkies (with the volume turned down reverentially low) contact continued between the respite volunteers in the chapel and the rescuers still with work to do at Ground Zero. And the priest spoke the words of institution. "This is my body. This is my blood".

It was the most powerful symbol, in its original sense of pulling together things which had been separated, of the unity of the *leitourgeia,* the performance of a public duty, and the *liturgy,* the expression of religious worship. It united the story in the first three gospels of the Lord's Supper with the St John's sacramental service of the foot-washing. And it became for me what Iona was for George MacLeod, "a thin place where only a piece of tissue paper separated the sacred from the secular."

Mayor Giuliani of New York described the survival of St Paul's Chapel as "a miracle". If he meant by that, any more than an expression of surprise and delight I would be worried, because a God who intervened to save a chapel but not six thousand people would have more than a few awkward questions to answer. However, granted that for whatever structural reasons, St Paul's Chapel survived, then by God's grace it became a "providential accident" in stone.

"Providential accident" is a phrase used by the great Jewish scholar Geza Vermez to describe his life-story. I think it is a very telling phrase to describe how we understand God works. He does not intervene to cause things to happen, but when they happen, he can use them inspirationally to evoke a response.

9

In May 2002 I reached the age of sixty, the age at which, ever since the days of John Reith, employees had to retire from the BBC. Maggie Cunningham, then Head of Radio, Scotland, agreed very willingly that I could stay on for a year for one day a week as a part-time consultant while I worked out what to do with the rest of my life.

I had moved my membership from the presbytery of Paisley to the presbytery of Ardrossan, where I hoped the church might find some use for me. Shortly after I retired, I was asked whether I would become interim moderator at a church in the presbytery which had recently become vacant, Barony St John's in the town of Ardrossan. I had a little knowledge of the congregation, which, for a variety of reasons, had experienced a number of relatively short ministries. I knew that the membership of the congregation had declined dramatically and that morale was extremely low. I had had some contact with members of the kirk session, whom I had found to be enthusiastic, committed but rather bruised. I said I would be happy to be interim moderator, and, at the first meeting of the kirk session, it was agreed that I should act as locum as well, initially for two days a week.

Such had been the immediate past history of the congregation that a committee of presbytery asked the office-bearers to consider whether this was a situation where an interim minister should be appointed. Interim Ministries had been a recent feature of the Church of Scotland. A group of ministers was appointed by the then Board of Ministry to go to congregations and parishes where it was felt their pastoral skills were needed, to resolve some situation or other, which required to be addressed before a regular minister was appointed. I had known a little of this work, because three people for whom I had a considerable respect, Jim Simpson, formerly minister of Dornoch Cathedral and moderator of the General Assembly, John Harvey, erstwhile leader of the Iona Community and Bernard Lodge who had exercised a significant ministry in St Columba's Kilmacolm, had all volunteered to become interim ministers and had done sterling work in a variety of different situations.

A group from the Board of Ministry visited the office-bearers and commended this form of ministry to Barony St John's, but pointed out that it would be at least a year or more before one could be allocated, even if the decision was that this parish was a suitable case. In those circumstances I was asked, with the approval of the presbytery clerk, to undertake a form of interim ministry, working with the congregation on a Sunday and four days a week. I started on the last Sunday in October 2002. What do you say to a congregation, bruised and battered, on your first Sunday with them? It seemed to me that one of the great themes of the bible is the theme of "exile". The people of Israel were to be perennial exiles; the New Testament describes us as "strangers and exiles here". So that was my theme, and to a tiny congregation that Sunday I said this:

"I've talked to enough of you to know that for quite some time a lot of you have felt that this church, where maybe you grew up, which maybe you decided to join, where for whatever reason you have felt at home, was somewhere you felt had changed. Things were happening you didn't like, or being said you couldn't agree with. And this place wasn't the same any more, and you felt in a kind of way in exile.

Robert Louis Stevenson spent the last years of his life in exile on the island of Samoa – for the good of his health. Out of the blue someone sent him a copy of a book which had been dedicated to him, and he sat down and wrote a poem which reflected the pain and the longing of the exile far from home:

Blows the winds today, and the sun and the rain are flying,
Blows the wind on the moors today and now,

Where about the graves of the martyrs the whaups are crying,
    My heart remembers how.

An exile looking back to the home far away. But exile isn't just a matter of geography.

A generation after Robert Louis Stevenson, the writer J M Barrie, of Peter Pan fame was looking back on growing up in the town of Kirriemuir. He said that our lives are a book in which we mean to write one story but in fact we write another. So we are in exile, separated from our hopes and dreams and ambitions.

Those of us who are getting on a bit, when we listen to our children talking about the kind of lives they lead or the sort of things they take for granted, or the situations where they don't bat and eyelid but would leave us speechless, ... these moments make us realise that our children's world isn't ours, and however much we may love them we aren't at home there, and to be truthful the reverse is true too. Our children sometimes listen to us and they wonder which planet we are on. There is something universal, which strikes an echo with all of about this theme of exile… about feeling that we're not at home. Which is why the theme of exile runs through the bible: Adam and Eve in exile from Paradise; Abraham in exile from his homeland, journeying to a future he knows nothing about; Moses in exile with the slaves in Egypt; the people of Jerusalem taken into exile in Babylon; Jesus – no sooner born than he is taken into exile in Egypt.

So if you have felt a kind of exile from your church here, then let's recognise that you're in good company. It's been the story of God's people down all the ages.

So what can it mean for the congregation of Barony St John's that the sense of exile some of us have felt has been shared with the long, long story of the people of faith?

It means first of all that our sense of exile should be a place of protest. We're right to be sad, to be regretful, to want it to be different. "Rage, rage, rage against the dying of the light" said the Welsh poet, Dylan Thomas.

Two hundred years ago, in the far north of Scotland, people whose families had lived on crofts for generations were suddenly evicted, told the land was no longer theirs to farm. The great glens, the straths, which had echoed to the sound of communities living and working and laughing together, fell silent, as the people were moved to the coast, or south to the cities or across the Atlantic. One version of Christian faith told them that this must be the will of God so they should accept it meekly and humbly and willingly. Another version of Christian faith told those who were throwing the people off the land that they were wrong, and encouraged the people at every turn to protest against this exile that was being imposed on them. For many of these people it was the bible which showed them how to protest at their exile.

Do you remember the people of Israel in Babylon, taunted by their captors to entertain them in their exile. "Go on! Sing us some of your songs." But that would have been to collude, to co-operate, to compromise with those who had taken them into exile. "No, we'll not. How can we sing the Lord's song in a strange land?" So if you have felt yourself in exile, then you were right to protest. But if our exile is only a place of protest, then we'll get stuck in the past: either stuck in the past out of nostalgia, or stuck in a past where what we remember are the wrongs and the pain and the frustration. And in that kind of past we're like Tam o' Shanter's wife – nursing our wrath to keep it warm.

And so after it has been a place of protest our exile must move on and become a place of presence. Let us stay with these Jewish exiles in Babylon unable to sing the Lord's song in a foreign land. Why? Well, because it was a foreign land and God was back home in Jerusalem, back there in the temple, back where they had always known God was. And then something strange happened. These exiles began to discover that God was with them, and where they least expected to find him, in their lost-ness and their confusion and their homelessness and their exile, God was with them.

Almost exactly a year ago, I went to New York in the aftermath of September 11th to make some radio programmes. One of the people I spoke to was Dr Daniel Matthews whose church was only a block or so away from the Twin Towers. He told me that until September 11th, American Christians had believed that the sign that God was with them was their success, that the proof of God's presence was their prosperity, that the evidence of God's favour was how thriving they were.

Now we're having to learn, he told me, to cope with the God who didn't prevent the suffering but still was there, right with them in the middle of it. If you've felt yourself to be in exile, I hope you sensed God's presence with you. God with us, God strangely in love with us. And so our exile moves from a place of protest, to a place of presence, and then it becomes a place of promise.

But be very, very clear what the promise is. It is not that everything will be all right tomorrow It is not that all the difficulties and problems will disappear. It is not that things are bound to get better. It is simply the promise. "I will be with you to the end of time."

Christ is alive! No longer bound
To distant years in Palestine
He comes to claim the here and now
And dwell in every place and time.

Let me end with a true story.

One of the great ministers of the nineteenth century was Norman MacLeod, minister of the Barony Church in Glasgow. One year a minister from Aberdeenshire was hauled before the General Assembly because he had dared to allow a layman, someone other than a minister, speak from his pulpit.

Norman MacLeod thought this was nonsense, and he said, so but he was almost alone. He was very depressed that the Church should be so short-sighted. So he went straight home and wrote a hymn that we're going to sing in a moment or two:

Courage, brother, do not stumble
Though thy path be dark as night
There's a star to guide the humble
Trust in god and do the right.

But he wrote a verse that nobody has put into the hymn books but maybe it should be there:

Trust no party, church or faction,
Trust no leaders in the fight,
But in every word and action
Trust in God and do the right."

In Barony St John's I found myself back in Bellahouston Steven again. The ambitious young minister, who had been desperate for a big pulpit like Paisley Abbey, had seen how empty that kind of ambition can be. The broadcaster, who had loved almost every minute of his time at the BBC, had come back to his first love, a parish and congregation. And the preacher, who had never quite lost the passion for preaching, had found it again.

Ardrossan is a place which has been the victim of the collapse of the shipbuilding industry. Whenever it is announced that the voting is to take place for the town which is to be declared "carbuncle of the year", then Ardrossan is there in the short leet. To be fair, it is not a place of scenic beauty, but the congregation, where I was asked to be a minister, is as fine a congregation as there is in the Church of Scotland.

Slowly, people who had stayed away from church began to return. Gradually the finances started to improve. And I began to find the sort of satisfaction in the ministry that Bellahouston Steven had inspired and Paisley Abbey all but destroyed.

The moment I knew I was accepted and at home was the Christmas shortly after I had started to work in Barony St John's. It was the Sunday School evening called "Carols by Candlelight". Evelyn and I arrived just before half-past seven, not entirely sure what to expect. There was a good crowd. Maybe eighty or ninety people seated at tables, the Sunday School getting into performance mode, and a Salvation Army tambourine band in an adjoining hall. "Where do you want us to sit?" I asked one of the Sunday School leaders. "Johnston, you can park your arse wherever you like" she replied. Instantly I knew I was at home!

Before I became involved with Barony St John's, I had been asked to take four Advent services in a congregation I had come to know and love in Edinburgh. (My friends will think "know and love in Edinburgh" is an example of McKay oxymoron!) Canonmills Baptist Church meets in what was Robert Louis Stevenson's primary school. Twenty years or so ago, when it became vacant, one of its leading lights, the great Scots actor Tom Fleming, consulted two friends about how it should face the future. One was the St Andrews theologian James Whyte, who had known Tom from schooldays, and the other was my old Assembly reporting colleague, Vernon Sproxton. The result was that the congregation decided not to call a minister. It would attend to the pastoral needs of the congregation from within its membership, led inspirationally by Tom Fleming, and it would invite visiting preachers from different denominations to conduct worship each Sunday. For several years, during my time at the BBC, I had preached in Canonmills on the two Sundays around the General Assembly, which gave me a base, and, latterly, allowed me to cook for the teams who were producing the programmes for which I was responsible but no longer actively involved in producing.

Tom Fleming had asked me if I would conduct Advent services in Canonmills in the year 2002, and I had agreed. So at my first meeting with the kirk session of Barony St John's, I explained that I had agreed to do this, but there was a problem. There was due to be a quarterly communion service on the first Sunday of December, the first Sunday of Advent. I explained that I thought there would be people attending communion that Sunday who, perhaps, hadn't been to church for some time, and I really wanted to get the chance to speak to them.

I had intended, gently, to suggest that perhaps the communion service might be changed to another day when the session clerk, Bobby Denver, as rough a diamond as you are likely to meet but, if it isn't too much of a mixed metaphor, with a heart of gold as well as a will of steel, said "No problem. We'll have the communion on the last Sunday in November".

End of discussion. I knew not only that I was at home but that this was a congregation which did not regard difficulties ever as insuperable!

So I preached in Canonmills, but I asked Tom Fleming on one of those Advent Sundays that if ever he revived his one-man show about George MacLeod, which he had performed so brilliantly in the Assembly Hall and elsewhere, he would bring it to Barony St John's. Six months later, the packed hall of Barony St John's had Tom Fleming on an improvised stage. Members of churches from far and wide came to be part of the audience. Barony St John's members proudly welcomed them all. Over £1000 was raised. But more than that, some of God's people in Ardrossan began to sense that the exile was over.

It was the experience of conducting worship in Canonmills, and getting to know the congregation, and its history, that convinced me that the Church of Scotland needs to do more lateral thinking about the need for full-time ministry. As I have written earlier, all the church's planning is based on the assumption that the only way for the local church to be church is to have a full time minister. Of course, lip service is paid to the need and the value of a wider understanding of ministry, but the bottom line is always that these are to complement or supplement the full time ordained ministry. And I now think that is nonsense. It rests on a number of assumptions.

First of all, there is an assumption that there are special things which only ordained ministers can do, principally conducting the sacraments of baptism and the Lord's Supper, I find it difficult now to understand why a baptism service or a communion service conducted by a competent member of a congregation, invited by the congregation to perform such ceremonies, should be less valid than ones conducted by an ordained minister. I wonder whether it is not time for that assumption to be questioned. For far too long, the Church of Scotland has allowed its life to be dictated by unchallenged assumptions like that.

Secondly, the need for every congregation to relate in some way to a full-time ministry rests on the assumption that the model of leadership which the ordained ministry offers is the only, or even the best one, and so one to which all others must relate. But as I have indicated already, I think that while the intrusion of a minister from outside the community where he or she is called to serve can provide an important source of objective, critical assessment of the life of a congregation, it frequently leads to the congregation becoming the creation of the minister's approach and attitudes. I am all in favour of critical, objective assessments of the pastoral needs of parishes, but that is precisely what presbyteries were set up to provide.

Thirdly the centrality of an ordained ministry rests on the assumption that the ordained ministry provides the theologically educated core of the church's teachers. But as I have also indicated, the level of theological education expected has decreased dramatically in the years since I was ordained. Many congregations contain people educated to a far higher level than the minister. And for far too long the assumption has been that in relation to theology the word "education" means putting into people's minds what is not there, whereas the original meaning of the word education was a drawing out from people of what is already there. Increasingly we need to allow what the people of God already know and believe to emerge.

At the time of writing I have spent exactly three years in Barony St John's. They could not have been happier or more fulfilling. And much of what I have written here has been the result of reflecting in and with that worshipping congregation.

In September 2003, the clerk of the presbytery of Ardrossan, David Broster, died. A few weeks later I was approached by some members of the presbytery to ask whether I would be willing to become the presbytery clerk. After discussion with friends, some of whom told me, in no uncertain terms, that in a daft life this was the daftest thing they had heard me suggest, I agreed to allow my name to be considered by the presbytery's Business committee which decided to submit my name for the approval of presbytery. I took up the post on 1 December 2003 on the basis that it would require a day each week to perform the duties.

Two days after I was appointed presbytery clerk, I received a letter from the session clerk of a congregation in Kilwinning, informing me that the congregation intended to secede from the Church of Scotland! That letter began a long process of legal wrangling, which, two years later is still going on.

Presbyteries were originally intended to oversee the work of the church in an area. Just as the church before the reformation had bishops, whose function was to supervise the pastoral care of an area, presbyteries were instituted to be the equivalent of the bishop, overseeing the provision for the pastoral needs of the parishes within the bounds of the presbytery. One of the results of the gradual centralising of the administration of the church has been that the pastoral function of the presbytery has diminished as its administrative function has increased. Occasionally I have the impression that the presbytery is viewed mainly as a conduit through which instructions can be passed from the central administration to the parishes.

My uncle, Kenneth MacVicar, once told me that as a presbytery clerk he invariably wrote the minutes of the meeting before it took place. That is not as strange as it sounds. The presbytery agenda is known in advance, and it is sensible to draft a minute on the assumption that what is being proposed is going to be approved. If someone challenges a proposal and moves an alternative one, then it is very easy to insert that into the draft which has been prepared. And not everything that is proposed is going to be challenged. Since so many people require to be informed quickly of presbytery decisions, Assembly committees, congregations affected by a decision, and many others, having the minute in draft form in advance allows extract minutes to be sent very quickly. I suspect the word processor, with the ability to "cut and paste" is the greatest boon to presbytery clerks since the invention of the typewriter. I have not yet copied the example of the clerk to the presbytery of the Western Cape in South Africa, sitting with his laptop amending the draft minute as the meeting progressed so that his minute was completed when the presbytery meeting ended. But it won't be long, I suspect! Ironically the first item of business at that presbytery meeting, ten thousand miles away was ... a congregation which wished to secede!

I was in South Africa because Alison Elliot asked me to be one of her chaplains when she was appointed moderator-designate in October 2003. Shortly after Alison became convener of the Church and Nation committee (frequently and amusingly referred to as "powerful and influential" though it has no power and its influence is felt much more outside the church than within it) I had been invited to become a member of the committee. It was obvious to anyone who sat on the committee that Alison was a person of quite exceptional ability. Her grasp of events, and mastering of the issues in the wide ranging topics which the committee covered, and her brilliant presentation of the reports to the Assembly won admiration. In the course of time I became involved in writing draft reports, and the consultation involved meant that I got to know Alison better. It also introduced me to her rigorous questioning of every point made, and refusal to allow a single word which could not be justified to appear in a report which she was going to have to defend on the floor of the General Assembly. That in turn led me to ask her to do some broadcasting, and as a contributor and presenter she became very accomplished extremely quickly. And our friendship grew. So I had been involved in conversations with her before she took the decision to allow her name to be proposed, and very soon after she was nominated she asked if I could help her as a chaplain during her year. Alison's husband Jo was not going to be able to be with her on every visit, and so Sheilagh Kesting, her other chaplain, and I would need to become more involved throughout the year than chaplains usually are. I accompanied Alison on the visits to the Presbyteries of Aberdeen and Paisley and Greenock, while Sheilagh was with her in the Presbyteries of Lewis and the Borders. Sheilagh joined Alison to Czechoslovakia and Poland, while I went to South Africa.

The reason that the Church's Board of World Mission had asked the moderator to go to South Africa was to mark the tenth anniversary of the first free elections there, and the fifth anniversary of the union between the largely white Presbyterian Church of South Africa and the predominantly black Reformed Presbyterian Church. The union had encountered difficulties between the formal, legal structure of the former and the much more informal and discursive style of the latter. White Presbyterians were used to presbytery meetings being presented with motions, amendments, countermotions and procedurally controlled debate, reaching decisions by a majority. Black Presbyterians preferred their way of "indebe", far longer discussion arriving at a decision only when a consensus has been reached.

In the two weeks or so we spent in South Africa, we were well aware of the tensions that existed, but it was not clear what a moderator from Scotland was meant to do about them: just listen?

A good many of the engagements which Alison was expected to fulfil were to historic sites associated with Scots missionaries of the past. At the initial meeting with the officials of one presbytery, we were told that they had been informed that this was what the moderator most wanted to see. Nothing could have been further from the truth! Alison Elliot's involvement with the church outside her own congregation has always been at the places where the church engages with society. She was, after all, the Associate Director of the Centre for Theology and Public Issues. Yet when we arrived in South Africa and eventually saw something which might approximate to a programme for the visit, there was hardly an engagement which reflected that interest. The only planned visit to any place connected with South Africa's dreadful AIDS experience was one which Alison asked to be included in the programme, to an area near the border with Zimbabwe, where the presbytery of Greenock had raised money to build a school for AIDS orphans. In the event we managed to make considerable changes to the programme, and saw some very exciting, moving projects to help the poor. But this owed nothing to the forward planning that had, presumably, been discussed when the General Secretary of the Board of World Mission, who also accompanied Alison on the trip, paid an earlier visit to South Africa to discuss arrangements for the visit.

There must have been five or six hundred people at the service on the Sunday morning in the church near where the school was being built by money from Scotland. It was hot. The slow rhythm of the fans in the roof captured the attention more than they circulated the air. Old Scots psalm tunes had been sung to words in Zulu. There had been a good deal of dancing. The moderator of the Kirk's General Assembly had preached and her sermon had been translated by an interpreter and captured on the video which was being made of the service.

It was an hour and three quarters after the service began, and I was about to begin celebrating communion, when the local minister said to me that there were just a few domestic matters to be dealt with first. He moved to the steps in front of the communion table and two women came from their seats and stood in front of him. He said that the kirk session had met the previous day, found them guilty of sins they knew they had committed, and banned them from communion until the kirk session decided they had served their punishment.

I turned to the church official sitting next to me, who knew the church well, for he had once been minister there. "That was dreadful" I said. "Yes" he answered slowly. "That's what your ancestors left to us, Johnston". Later we asked whether it was always women who were dealt with in this manner and were told that it was. What of the men? Oh, they were dealt with privately.

If that is the most chilling memory of our visit to South Africa, the most moving was a visit to what had been a shop in a poor suburb of East London. An elder in a local church had rented the shop, without enough money to pay for the first month or two's rent. Inside there was a bright foyer where we met Rosemary and three nurses. They had all given up their paid jobs to work with those dying of AIDS. Such is the stigma attached to the disease that, although early treatment is available, people leave it till too late to admit what is wrong with them. Behind a partition, four women lay dying on spotless sheets in a dark 'ward', tended with tangible love: so dark and so loving that it reminded me of Malcolm Muggeridge describing wanting to film in Mother Theresa's House of the Dying, and being told by his cameraman that there was not nearly sufficient light. Nothing would register. But Muggeridge asked the cameraman to film anyway, and back home, when developed, everything was as clear as daylight on the film.

Part of the darkness of the AIDS pandemic is the stigma and the failure to agree to early testing. When someone proposed at the General Assembly of the Uniting Presbyterian Church that everyone there should take a test as an act of witness, the motion was defeated.

In what had been the great missionary college at Lovedale, now municipally owned, a project had been established to teach local women basic sewing. With little money, they would be able to make, not buy, clothes for their families. Those women with the greatest aptitude moved on to produce academic gowns and hoods, or tracksuits, and learn basic business skills that would allow them to generate an income. The project was creative, imaginative and effective, and inspired by a missionary and his wife.

Elsewhere we saw churches where young people were creating their own music to attempt to destroy myths about AIDS, where facilities and a tiny amount of capital had been provided for a man who painstakingly produced a few bricks to sell each day, and visited the foundations of that school which will be built for the orphans of AIDS by congregations in the west of Scotland.

It is such a strange amalgam, the Church, all our churches: at once judgmental and sacrificially loving, fearful and creative.

So how did the communion service begin in that church where judgment had been passed on the women who the minister called "fallen sinners"? I tried to produce an appropriate version of what the liturgists call "the gracious invitation", and said that St Paul wrote that we had all sinned and fallen short of the glory of God, and so this was a sacrament for sinners, a feast for the fallen. But by then the women I wanted to hear the words had left.

As well as looking after Barony St John's, and being presbytery clerk, and, for a year, the moderator's chaplain, I continued to be asked to broadcast. The series of *Personal Touch* programmes continued, though no longer throughout the year. I still contributed to *Thought for the Day* and other programmes both for Radio Scotland and Radio 4.

Thought for the Day was religious broadcasting's showcase in BBC Radio Scotland's flagship programme, *Good Morning Scotland*. When I joined BBC Scotland, *Thought for the Day* was almost exclusively Christian. Very quickly we started to involve people from the faith communities. The policy was that in two minutes, people were expected to address an issue of the day, or the mood of the day from their religious perspective. And we asked these contributors to prepare and deliver their scripts in a way that did not stand out like a sore thumb in a fast-moving, pacy news programme.

The problem was that those who were responsible for the production of *Good Morning Scotland* did not really want *Thought for the Day* to relate to the rest of the programme. If it did, then it was likely to impinge on their news agenda. Most of them wanted *Thought for the Day*, if it had to exist at all (and the vast majority of *Good Morning Scotland* producers wanted rid of it) to be pious, spiritual, ineffectual and unrelated to anything round about it on the programme. Meanwhile we were trying to persuade contributors to be alert, topical, relevant and fit into everything round about them on the programme.

When I left the BBC I continued to contribute, but I began to notice a distinct change in the style of contributions, especially when Anna Magnusson, who had been appointed Senior Producer in religious broadcasting when I left, took a career break. A far wider range of contributors appeared, who seemed not to relate to the news of the day. "Themed weeks" on the slot became fashionable, indicating that topicality and religious insight into current events was less important than lateral planning for some contrived theme.

In the summer of 2005, about six o'clock one evening, while on holiday, I was telephoned by a friend, who was also a contributor to *Thought for the Day*, to be told that the slot was to be moved from 7.25 am to 6.50 am. I immediately wrote a letter to *The Scotsman* and *The Herald*, criticising this decision, pointing out that the Scottish Religious Advisory committee, which is appointed by the Broadcasting Council for Scotland to advise it on religious matters, had not been informed of this plan even although it had met just a few weeks before. BBC Scotland announced that it would temporarily reinstate *Thought for the Day* at 7.25, but a few weeks later it announced that the change of time would take effect. I quickly contacted as many contributors as I could and got their agreement to sign a letter which, again, asked for discussions with the Advisory committee and perhaps contributors. Shortly afterwards BBC Scotland announced that there would be no change of time until the Advisory committee had met. Shortly afterwards a meeting of contributors was arranged.

I was not entirely surprised when I got a letter, a few weeks later, to say that the series of *Personal Touch* programmes was not to return. I was told that this was because it had been decided that some speech programmes had to be given to Inverness, presumably on the basis that there were not sufficient programmes coming from Inverness for it to pay its post-Birtian way. If I was not entirely sure that was the real reason, it is probably because people trained in history have suspicious minds, always unwilling to accept facts as presented until they can be confirmed. I was assured that this would not be a reduction in religious broadcasts as these programmes would still have a spiritual basis.

That last phrase was much more worrying to me than the loss of involvement with *Personal Touch*. When I joined the BBC, Ian Mackenzie's policy was that what mattered was whether producers could make good programmes, not whether or not they were signed up to any religious community. I certainly continued that policy. But I now wonder: did that policy of using the best producers to make religious programmes rest on two assumptions: one, that BBC management was, on the whole, sympathetic to and supportive of religious broadcasting, and, two, that although there may be a number of individual producers who themselves could not confess to any religious faith, there was someone at the helm who could? Programmes are not religious simply because their content is religious. That may be the case, but genuinely religious programmes, those which communicate in a lively, tangential, evocative, seductive way the religious dimension to life require that someone be involved at the editorial level who understands the subtleties and ambiguities of religious faith. And I have yet to be convinced that in a BBC Scotland which now has no dedicated Religious Broadcasting Department either in television or on radio, that can be guaranteed.

But, as I have said about ministers and parishes, periods in religious broadcasting live only for their time. And as the year 2005 draws to a close, I believe that the time has come for me to stop broadcasting as much as I have, not only because there is a new generation of producers with different views and standards from those who had brought me into the BBC, but because religious broadcasting has moved on, and so have I. The fulcrum of my interest has altered and I am much more involved with the church than I ever imagined I would be again. I am totally fulfilled in what I am doing. For a number of reasons I am happier than I have ever been.

It is time to move on, but with more thanks than I can express to my families for all they have put up with, to colleagues in the BBC who gave me more professional satisfaction than I knew existed, and to my closest friends. Willie Barclay used to say that he was fortunate "granted who I am, that I have the friends I do".

I can echo that.